LUTHERANS
OF
COLE COUNTY,
MISSOURI
A History

Jeremy P. Ämick

THE
History
PRESS

Published by The History Press
Charleston, SC
www.historypress.com

Front cover: Zion Lutheran Church was established in 1843 south of Jefferson City and became the "Mother Church" to other Lutheran congregations in the county. *Jeremy P. Ämick.*

First published 2023

Manufactured in the United States

ISBN 9781467154895

Library of Congress Control Number: 2023937174

To the memory of the brave, pioneering immigrants who came to Cole County from Germany beginning in the 1830s. Your hard work and vision have not been forgotten while we continue to reap the benefits of your sacrifices.

We are forever grateful.

CONTENTS

ACKNOWLEDGEMENTS

It was quite the undertaking to weave together the tangled web connecting the various Lutheran churches in Cole County, while at the same time making sense of the individual stories of German immigration that emerged in the process. First, let me extend my gratitude to the late Gert Strobel, whose research and documentation of history has been invaluable. Also, my appreciation goes out to all the members of the various Lutheran churches and others in the county who have been more than willing to assist me in this process, such as: Schellie Blochberger, Paul Junkans, Gary and Doris Schmutzler, Pastor Gerald Scheperle, Patty Ott, Stan Linsenbardt, Rev. Warren Brandt, June Nivens, Candace Stockton, Susan Scheperle Schnewerk, Pastor David Viles, Bonnie Mae Rau, Randy Deuschle, Gus and Jeanette Fischer, Harry Thompson, Dr. Roger Jungmeyer, Jack and Bethel Johnson, the Schmoeger family, Walter Schroeder, Larry Meisel and Henry Gensky…and a host of others I may have unintentionally overlooked. Each and every one of you is appreciated and has contributed in some way to this book by sharing photographs, stories, historical documents and, in some cases, words of encouragement. *Vielen Dank an euch alle!*

INTRODUCTION

This history of the Lutheran Church and several German Evangelical congregations in Cole County is a story that parallels an immigration legacy beginning shortly after Missouri achieved statehood in 1821. Arriving in the New World, these families originating from the various regions that later became part of the German nation helped expand the boundaries of the United States westward. Often settling along the rivers and waterways, which, in retrospect, represented the major highways of the period, they helped the St. Louis area develop into a centralized representation of industrialization in the West.

During the 1830s, many Lutheran families journeyed to Jefferson City and worked to establish their homes among those with common backgrounds and religious beliefs. Only a few years earlier, on October 1, 1826, Jefferson City had been designated the capital of Missouri, and at the time, it was home to only a few dozen families and a small collection of businesses. Census records from the early period of the county's history reveal names predominantly associated with Western European origins. This began to shift with the penning of a publication broadly distributed by a German native that touted the possibilities available in the expansive hinterlands of Missouri.

Born in 1789 in the Duchy of Berg, a former state in the Rhineland of Germany, Gottfried Duden's father owned an apothecary business and imbued in his son an analytical and inquisitive bearing. The younger Duden would go on to study law, work in government positions and then, along with many of his peers during this period of history, serve in the infantry in campaigns during the Napoleonic Wars. Following his release from military commitments, Duden developed an unyielding interest in the establishment of new settlements overseas while also pursuing a higher education by studying medicine and sociology subjects at the University of Bonn.

"On the 8th of June, 1824, accompanied by only one companion, Louis Eversmann, an expert agriculturist, Gottfried Duden set sail from his own country on an American sailship [sic], the Henry Clay, arriving in Baltimore August 14," explained the Kansas City Star in an article printed August 23, 1923. "Traveling in an open spring wagon, Duden and his traveling companion went through Wheeling [West Virginia], Zanesville, Chillicothe and Cincinnati in Ohio, Louisville [Kentucky], and finally arrived at St. Louis the latter part of October 1824."

The German pioneer applied his scientific interests by purchasing property in Warren County to conduct agricultural experiments and collect sociological observations of the area. After nearly three years in Missouri, he returned to his homeland and purportedly penned a collection of thirty-six letters to a friend describing his pioneering experiences in Missouri. In 1829, these letters were published in a book that detailed his emigration experiment under the title Bericht über eine Reise nach den westlichen Staaten Nordamerika's [Report on a Journey to the Western States of North America]. This popular and widely read publication detailed the advantages of living in Missouri and asserted that this new land was absent many of the problems faced by those living in Germany, such as high taxes, corrupt government and unaffordable or unavailable property. Although Duden was accused by some of embellishing his experiences in Missouri and purportedly painting a false picture for his fellow countrymen, his book served as a rousing invitation for an estimated 120,000 Germans who immigrated to the United States in the 1830s; one-third of this new immigrant population reportedly chose to settle in Missouri.

Through his busy pen, Duden described the Missouri landscape: "Many times I have said to myself and to my traveling companion (whom I shall leave behind in the most fortunate situation): People in Europe will not and cannot believe how easy and how pleasant it can be to live in this country. It sounds too strange, too fabulous. Believing in similar places on this earth has too long been consigned to the fairy-tale world."

Interestingly, despite any plans he may have had, Duden never returned to Missouri and spent the remainder of his days in Germany. On his death in 1856, he still retained ownership of the farm he had purchased in Missouri.

On the heels of Duden's influential writings came the establishment of the Giessen Emigration Society in 1833. This society came about when Friedrich Muench and Paul Follenius, residents of Giessen, Germany, both of whom had attended university together, published a pamphlet encouraging a mass migration to the United States.

"Prompting the emigration from Germany was much more than an ordinary desire for change or physical betterment," wrote Walter B. Stevens in the *Centennial History of Missouri: 1820–1921*. "Here was the ardent aspiration for political freedom which Duden had pictured so forcibly as existing in Missouri. These Giesseners were men and women with ideals. The men were leaders of higher education."

An estimated five hundred brave and pioneering souls, finding comfort and hope in the ideals promulgated by the Giessen Emigration Society, pulled up their roots in Germany and traveled to Missouri in 1834 to establish a new colony. With many settling in areas west of St. Louis, including St. Charles, Warren and Franklin Counties, the society disbanded a short time later. Its members' lives as new Americans continued to unfold, and many who had carried with them their faiths, such as Lutheranism, moved farther west down the Missouri River and joined others working to establish a foothold in Jefferson City and surrounding areas.

Inspiring what appeared to many living in Missouri as a mass exodus from Germany, this represented the beginning of a revolutionary period for the young state. Beginning in the 1830s, the European nation experienced poor working conditions, growing levels of unemployment and failed harvests, the latter of which was followed by ever-increasing food and commodity prices. From this came several revolts contributing to the overall misery experienced by the general working-class population. These revolutions continued and, in the coming years, stimulated subsequent waves of immigration to Cole County and eventually resulted in the development and growth of such communities as Zion, Stringtown and Lohman.

The descriptions of Missouri written by a relatively unknown individual thrust into the limelight the expressions of Duden, along with the dreams of the Giessen Society founders, and resonated greatly among many in Germany seeking better circumstances. As James E. Ford explained in *A History of Jefferson City, Missouri's State Capital, and of Cole County*, "A steady stream of immigration from Germany, beginning in volume about 1830 and continuing for several decades, exercised a marked influence in the development of the young American nation; Jefferson City and Cole County received the full tide of this immigration. It was limited to certain areas, one of which bearing the strongest appeal being the area adjacent to the Missouri River from the central portion of the state to its mouth."

The early German settlements around the Jefferson City area began to grow as families arrived in the area, established their farms and businesses and then wrote to relatives and acquaintances back in Europe, encouraging them to also consider the promises offered by living in Missouri.

As Walter A. Baepler explains in *A Century of Grace*, although the Germans arriving in the Jefferson City area were filled with hope and ambition in this new land of opportunity, the hardships they encountered often were not accompanied by an initial emphasis on nurturing their Lutheran faith. In sharing the writings of Pastor Friedrich Wyneken, who traveled with a group of these hopeful emigrants leaving Saxony and bound for the United States in the late 1830s, Baepler states, "Alas, Bible and hymnal also in many cases have been left in the Old Country, as the people, owing to rationalism, had lost taste for them. No preacher arrives to rouse them from their carnal thoughts and pursuits, and the sweet voice of the Gospel has not been heard for a long time."

"Among the German immigrants of the 1830s were three major religious groups: the Catholics…, members of the Reformed Evangelical Church of Germany, and the Saxon Lutherans," shares Duane Meyer in *The Heritage of Missouri: A History*. But describing a major change in the development of Lutheranism, Meyer continues, "In 1839, a group of 600 Lutherans from the German province of Saxony came to Missouri under the leadership of Martin Stephan. Although some remained in St. Louis where they accepted the gracious invitation to use Christ Church as their first temporary church, most settled to the south in Perry County where they established Altenburg and Wittenberg."

The Saxon immigration of 1839 had the greatest influence on the Lutheran congregations that soon began to grow in Cole County, Missouri. The grand wave of immigration, which had for the most part been represented by individuals or small families choosing to leave their homelands, was not characteristic of this group. These Lutherans, often arriving as part of larger settlements, "came to America not to gain more of this world's goods than they were able to acquire in the land of their birth, but to seek freedom of conscience; they did not come as hunters of fortune, but because they desired a better country, that is a heavenly one," writes Professor Theo Bueger in *Ebenezer: Reviews of the Work of the Missouri Synod during Three Quarters of a Century*. "Spiritual freedoms denied back in their German homeland had driven them to Missouri where they sought to instead build their fortunes in heaven," he continues. Following their immigration, "[t]he church-body that was later formed by them, their doctrinal position, their congregational church government, their principles of Christian life and morality...still exert an influence upon...people in the United States." On a more local level, this immigration continues to have an impact in the lives of their descendants—the Lutheran families of Cole County.

Martin Stephan emerged as a leader of this group of early Lutheran immigrants but was exiled to Illinois following charges of unscrupulous behavior, including the mishandling of funds after squandering the collective treasury of his fellow colonists on personal items and his own household. Dr. Carl Ferdinand Wilhelm Walther, a Lutheran minister and Saxon immigrant living in St. Louis, was unexpectedly selected to lead this group of God's faithful and dedicated servants. In a few years, they would go on to form the German Evangelical Lutheran Synod of Missouri, Ohio and Other States (Die Deutsche Evangelisch-Lutherische Synode von Missouri), later known as the Missouri Synod. In 1847, Walther became the first general president of the Lutheran Church—Missouri Synod. Other ministers who were part of this original group of immigrants that came to Missouri from Germany with Walther later had influential roles in the formation of Lutheran congregations in Cole County, the first being the historic Zion Lutheran Church near Jefferson City.

And with the establishment of Zion Lutheran Church, the proverbial mustard seed grew into a mighty network of thriving Lutheran and German Evangelical congregations throughout Cole County and the surrounding areas. The small congregation at Zion, founded by thirty-seven immigrants, quickly sprouted into a new congregation in nearby Lohman, which then suffered a doctrine-based rift after the Civil War that resulted in the formation of another Lutheran church in Stringtown. Other congregations began to grow in sections of the county to include churches in Schubert near Taos, Russellville, Honey Creek, Centertown and Jefferson City. Some descendants of these early Lutheran immigrants also helped found churches of other denominations in locations such as Osage Bluff, Jefferson City and Brazito.

It is a legacy with many fascinating facets and familial ties, demonstrating the hardy and stalwart spirit of an immigrant population seeking a better life for themselves and their families. It also formed into a story of different branches of the Lutheran faith, such as the Missouri Synod and the former Iowa Synod, among others. These pioneering families brought their faith with them to this new, strange land called Cole County, and the churches they established have overwhelmingly weathered the years and continue to share the Gospel with many of their descendants in addition to new believers brought into the Lutheran fold.

Jeremy P. Ämick
Russellville, Missouri
May 2023

CHAPTER 1

ZION LUTHERAN CHURCH (JEFFERSON CITY)

The "Mother Church" of Lutheran Congregations in Cole County, Missouri

Gustav Wilhelm Loesch became one of many pioneering spirits who left the oppressions of their ancestral homeland to immigrate to the United States. The twenty-eight-year-old arrived in 1838 along with his new wife, Johanna Sophia Muller, and soon joined many of his fellow immigrants, predominantly from the German states of Bavaria and Saxony, who had settled in a small community near Jefferson City. They toiled to establish a new life, integrating into the social fabric of their rural Missouri surroundings while clinging to certain German traditions. One achievement came with the building of an edifice that continues to resonate with the story of their shared Lutheran faith, which came after several years of having no formal religious structure available for these immigrant families pouring into the area.

"The mother congregation of all area Lutheran churches, Zion's roots stem back to July 19, 1843," wrote the late Palmer Scheperle, a local historian. His records note that it was on this date that thirty-seven men met to organize the congregation of Zion Lutheran Church. It was two days later, on July 21, 1843, that this group, eager to begin erecting a house of worship, again met to decide on the piece of property where the church should be built.

Records maintained by descendants of the congregation note that this group of thirty-seven Christians consisted of: Johann Antweiler, Christopher Arnhold, Heinrich Beck, Heinrich Birkicht, Peter Blochberger, Gottlieb Deimler, Heinrich Duehafen, Adam Duenkel, Friedrich Eggers, Heinrich Eggers, Wilhelm Fischer, Peter Flessa, Christian Frantz, Karl Frisch, Johann

Zion Lutheran Church was established by German immigrants in 1843. Pictured is the third church building, dedicated in 1906. *Jeremy P. Ämick.*

N. Hahn, Adam Heisinger, Heinrich Heisinger, Andreas Holzbeierlein, Johann Peter Koch, Johann Lampe, Gustav Loesch, Johann Loesch, Paul Gottlieb Loesch, John Mersel, Johann Friedrich Meister, Wilhelm Mohr, John G. Peetz, George Plank, Johann Plank, Nikolaus Raithel, Johann

Heinrich Rockemann, Johann Christ Schochart, Johann Vogel, Christoph Wolf, Johann C. Wolfrum, Leonhard Wolfrum and Konrad Wunderlich. From this distinguished group, Gottlieb Diemler and Christian Frantz were chosen to serve as the first elders of the budding congregation.

The names of these pioneers are spelled as they appear in the one hundredth anniversary booklet of Zion Lutheran Church, printed in 1943. Records from other Lutheran churches in the area reveal variations in the spellings of some of these names. Some of these can be attributed the English pronunciation of German names (such as John instead of Johann). Other records note surnames as they came to be used in later years (such as Rockelman instead of Rockemann).

These three dozen men, many with families to raise, arrived in Missouri with limited economic resources, but several would, through their toils and labors, be able to build a more comfortable living for their families. They immersed themselves in the process of establishing their homes and families in a strange new land while also striving to ensure they could eventually unite to establish a house of worship with their fellow believers. Among this group of hardy pioneers were persons such as Christopher Arnhold, who went on to erect a successful mill in Camden County and establish the community of Brazito in addition to building a store and stable. This unique group of immigrants also included Wilhelm Mohr, half brother of Joseph Mohr, the Catholic priest who had penned the Christmas classic "Silent Night" more than two decades prior to the establishment of Zion Lutheran Church. Others who were counted among these founding members of the first Lutheran congregation in Cole County became parents to children who spread out into neighboring communities and helped establish Lutheran, German Evangelical and Methodist churches.

Embracing the collective desire of a small group of individuals seeking to form a Lutheran church, the fledgling congregation purchased property for their church a few miles southwest of Jefferson City on what is now Zion Road. A milestone moment occurred approximately two years after the congregation's founding, on July 22, 1845, when they dedicated a twenty-eight-by-thirty-six-foot structure hewn from logs that served as the first church. Prior to this, it is believed that the group met in the homes of families to share in their Lutheran faith despite the absence of a pastor. So many had toiled to make this rustic structure of worship a reality. This was a significant undertaking, since the funds to establish a new church had to come from the small congregation, whose members were just beginning to become economically integrated into the surrounding communities.

Gustav Wilhelm Loesch is pictured with his wife, Johanna Sophia Mueller. Loesch was a charter member of Zion Lutheran Church. *Candace Stockton.*

Additionally, there were no sawmills in the area, and the roofing of the new church structure was made of clapboards hand-split from locally harvested logs. A church historical booklet notes that a balcony was installed around three sections of the interior of the church to maximize the use of space. Focused on efficiency, economy and making use of the resources at their disposal, these talented and foresighted Germans also fashioned pews from timber cut from the surrounding forest. A number of their fellow German immigrants who had settled in Cole County were of the Catholic faith but maintained their shared Germanic legacy with their Lutheran brothers and sisters, thus finding ways to uphold their respective denominational uniqueness in this strange new land.

"One of the charter members of Zion (Lutheran) Church, [Johann] Antweiler, was of the Roman Catholic faith," Palmer Scheperle explains in some of his writings about the early beginnings of the Cole County

Dr. C.F.W. Walther became the first president of the Lutheran Church—Missouri Synod, when it was established in 1847. *St. John's Lutheran, Stringtown.*

church. "The 1870 U.S. Census notes the sixty-five-year-old Antweiler, a native of Prussia, was employed as a shoe manufacturer." Further explaining Antweiler's religious leanings, Scheperle adds, "It is not certain if he was the only one, but we are told that the Roman Catholics held mass on Saturday evenings and the Lutherans held services on Sunday morning in the first church building."

Some of these early Catholics who made use of the Lutheran church at Zion later moved to the eastern edge of Stringtown, where they founded the Catholic mission of St. Joseph's. All that remains of this mission is a small cemetery and the limestone foundation of what was once a small log church.

During Zion Lutheran Church's first five years, its members received spiritual guidance from traveling missionaries and circuit riders who served several small congregations. One problem associated with such a structure of spiritual support was that in the absence of an established synod, many of these pastors shared disparate biblical messages when it came to the Scriptures, oftentimes affirming doctrine not soundly rooted in the faith of their homeland since there was not a synodical education available on this new frontier. But finally, a twenty-year-old candidate named John Paul Kalb received the call to serve as the church's first official pastor. Shortly after his appointment to Zion in 1848, he was ordained a Lutheran minister.

Born on July 4, 1828, Kalb graduated from the Practical Seminary in St. Louis, and after moving to Cole County in 1848, he remained for the next four years. Local church histories note that his life as a minister in rustic central Missouri was filled with difficulties while he served not only Zion Lutheran Church but also other Lutheran communities, including the ones that had begun to form in Honey Creek, Jefferson City and Stringtown. Stories passed down through generations by members of the former Zion Lutheran Church note that Pastor Kalb often traveled to outlying rural areas by horseback and covered one hundred square miles of land, often in less-than-favorable road and weather conditions. In 1852, he traveled to the community that would years later be named Lohman, helping to establish St. Paul's Lutheran Church under the structure of the recently organized Missouri Synod.

In the spring of 1852, after taking an active leadership role in the organization of the new congregation in Lohman, the twenty-three-year-old Pastor Kalb accepted a call to serve a congregation in Lancaster, Ohio. A little more than six years later, on June 8, 1858, Pastor Kalb was but thirty years old when he became the victim of unfortunate tragedy, drowning. Following his death, he was buried in a Lutheran cemetery in Fort Wayne, Indiana.

As the years passed, to prepare pastors who would go on to serve congregations throughout Missouri and the western frontier, somewhat formalized training was conducted at a one-room log cabin built in 1839 in Altenberg in Perry County. This nondescript beginning education for Lutheran ministers served as the forerunner to Concordia Theological Seminary, which came into existence ten years later and continues to prepare Lutheran ministers for the Missouri Synod from educational institutions established in St. Louis and Fort Wayne, Indiana. Zion Lutheran Church predated the Missouri Synod by four years and in its early years operated as an independent Lutheran church. A few years after its founding, the congregation of Zion Lutheran Church joined the Missouri Synod and would, under this rather conservative doctrinal umbrella, go on to help establish other Missouri synod congregations in the county.

Zion then welcomed Carl William Reinhard Frederking as pastor in 1852. A native of Börninghause, Germany, located in the region of North Rhine-Westphalia, he was born on November 27, 1827, and later immigrated to the United States, settling in Missouri in 1850. He graduated from the Practical Lutheran School at Fort Wayne, Indiana, in 1852 and the same year married Christine Dorothea Charlotte Wunderlich in St. Louis. On April 28, 1852, he was installed to pastor the newly formed congregation at St. Paul's Lutheran Church in the community that would become known as Lohman approximately thirty years later. During the three years he served the Lutherans in central Missouri, he and his wife welcomed their first child, a son named Heinrich.

As part of his pastoral responsibilities, Frederking carried forth the legacy of his predecessor by serving not only the congregations at Zion and Lohman but also those continuing to develop in Honey Creek and Jefferson City. Pastor Frederking and his family resided in Stringtown but left the area in 1855 after receiving a call to Immanuel Lutheran Church in Olivette, Missouri. Sadly, his first wife later died, and Frederking remarried. He and his second wife would go on to have children together, but tragedy struck again when she died, resulting in Frederking's third marriage. Like many pastors of that era, he transferred to different congregations throughout his career, which included stints at churches in New Wells, Missouri, and eventually with the congregation at Goodfarm Trinity Lutheran Church in Grundy County, Illinois. The Lutheran minister passed away on November 22, 1902, and was laid to rest in the Goodfarm Cemetery in Grundy County, Illinois, alongside his wife and one of his daughters.

The background of those who were early pastors of Zion was generally reflective of the congregation they served, since most were recent immigrants to the United States. This list included Emil Julius Moritz Wege, who became the pastor at Zion Lutheran Church when he was installed in 1856. Again, like his predecessors, Wege also served other developing congregations in the area, such as St. Paul's in Lohman (then known as Stringtown). Born in Prussia on January 28, 1801, Wege was almost thirty-eight years old when he traveled from the port at Bremen, Germany, aboard the passenger ship *Olbers*, arriving in New Orleans on January 21, 1839, simply one immigrant among a large group of Lutherans. He had been a traveling companion of C.F.W. Walther, the man who would become the first president of the Missouri Synod in 1847.

Possessing a master of arts degree from his homeland, Wege was a candidate of theology on his arrival in America and was installed at his first church in late 1842, Holy Cross Lutheran Church in Cole Camp. The

following year, he married Meta Gefken, a native of Saxony. Like so many of his Lutheran contemporaries, Wege also helped establish and serve preaching stations in the Cole Camp area that later evolved into church bodies. He served the congregations in the vicinity of Cole Camp until 1855, at which time he moved to Cole County and embarked on his service predominantly at Zion Lutheran Church and St. Paul's Lutheran Church. Records maintained by St. John's Lutheran Church in Stringtown indicate that he also supported other growing Lutheran congregations in the area during his stint in Cole County. As previously noted, these supported congregations were located in Honey Creek and Jefferson City and would later become Immanuel Lutheran Church and Trinity Lutheran Church, respectively. But at

Emil Wege immigrated to the United States in 1839 and became one of the early pastors of Zion Lutheran Church. *St. Paul's Lutheran, Lohman.*

the time of Wege's spiritual support and guidance, these congregations had simply been founded and were yet to be officially organized.

While Pastor Wege was serving Zion Lutheran Church and also supporting St. Paul's in Lohman, dissension arose within the latter congregation in 1864, motivating many St. Paul's members to vocalize their desire to remove the congregation from the Missouri Synod. It was a tumultuous moment in the history of St. Paul's, which led to an argument over specifics of doctrine, thus resulting in a split and the formation of a new Lutheran congregation. The details of this unique historical occurrence are discussed in much greater detail in chapter 3, dedicated to the history of St. Paul's Lutheran Church in Lohman.

"Pastor Wege remained with Zion about one year after the troublous year of 1864," explains the historical booklet printed for the 150th anniversary of St. John's Lutheran Church in Stringtown. "The one other church which Pastor Wege served after he left Zion was the Christ Lutheran Church, Augusta, Missouri (1865–1870)," the booklet continues. Burial records indicate Reverend (a title bestowed on retired Lutheran pastors) Wege was sixty-nine years old when his spirit made the ascension on July 3, 1870, and was interred in the cemetery of Christ Lutheran Church in Augusta.

Hardships of life in a new settlement also resulted in the deaths of infants, young persons and the aged, necessitating a site for burials be established. The congregation at Zion chose to keep the bodies of their loved ones close by the church where they had worshiped and within the community around Zion Lutheran Church, thus designating a plot of land for a cemetery. Some historical accounts maintain that burials took place in what became the church cemetery prior to the organization of Zion Lutheran Church in 1843.

Youth soon demonstrated that it was not a prohibition against Christian leadership when the twenty-three-year-old Friedrich William Sandvoss, a German native, was installed as pastor of Zion Lutheran Church in 1865. Born in Erfurt, Germany, on February 28, 1842, he immigrated to Missouri and graduated from Concordia Seminary in St. Louis. In 1867, two years following his installation at Zion, Sandvoss helped organize St. John's Lutheran Church in Stringtown after the congregation split from St. Paul's Lutheran Church in Lohman over the previously mentioned doctrinal disputes.

Also during Sandvoss's tenure at Zion, the first church parsonage was erected in 1866 using timber and other materials from the area. It was also under his leadership that a Christian day school was organized,

The founders of Zion Lutheran Church designated a site for the cemetery around the time the church was organized in 1843. *Jeremy P. Amick.*

consisting of eight grades, which served nearly three dozen children in its first year (1865). His pastoral duties in Cole County came to an end in 1868, when he accepted a call to Ebenezer Lutheran Church in Leslie, Missouri, which continues to operate as a congregation of the Missouri Synod. Sandvoss went on to serve other Lutheran congregations and was leading a congregation in Appleton City, Missouri, when he passed away at only forty-five years of age in 1887.

"The Constitution for Zion Lutheran Church and for St. John's Lutheran Church was drawn up and written in German under the leadership of Pastor Sandvoss," explains the 150th anniversary booklet of St. John's Lutheran Church.

On August 9, 1868, a twenty-five-year-old Charles H.L. Thurow was installed as pastor at Zion, quickly becoming one of several central figures in the history of several area Lutheran churches. Thurow, like many of his predecessors and contemporaries, was born in Germany and immigrated with his parents to Wisconsin when he was but a young man. Developing an interest in becoming a man of the cloth, he attended seminary in St. Louis and graduated on June 13, 1868. The following day, Thurow accepted his official call to come serve the twenty-five-year-old congregation at Zion.

It was during his ministry at Zion Lutheran Church that Trinity Lutheran Church in Jefferson City and Immanuel Lutheran Church in Honey Creek were organized. Thurow, like his predecessor, continued to support the fledgling St. John's congregation in Stringtown while St. Paul's Lutheran Church in Lohman, now affiliated with the Synod of Iowa, had the resources to call and support its own pastor. Additionally, Thurow was one of the first Lutheran pastors in the area to be well versed in the English language, a proficiency that provided him opportunities in local education.

A booklet written by the congregation of Zion Lutheran Church in 1968 in celebration of its 125th anniversary explains of Thurow's bilingual abilities: "This afforded him an opportunity to teach in various public schools during his vacations." The booklet further notes, "At Zion he served both as Zion's parochial school teacher and its pastor, and during the summer continuing his public-school teaching….His next call was to lead him to Root Creek, Wisconsin. Here, besides his newly organized parish, he served as president of one of the Wisconsin Synod conferences, or districts." One of these local schools where he taught was the Zion public school, located about one mile east of the present church. This school closed in the early 1940s during the consolidation of local districts, but the school building still stands on privately owned property.

Rev. Thurow was seventy-two years old when he died on September 5, 1915, and is buried alongside his wife in Saint John's Evangelical Lutheran Church Cemetery in Milwaukee.

Between 1871 and 1872, the congregations at Zion and St. John's relied on seminary students to fill their pulpits until the arrival of Pastor A.H. Wetzel. This shared arrangement between St. John's in Stringtown and Zion came to an end with the arrival of Pastor Dietrich Friedrich Herman Wesche in

Pastor Charles Thurow was installed at Zion Lutheran Church in 1868 and later helped organize Trinity Lutheran Church in Jefferson City and Immanuel Lutheran Church in Honey Creek. *Trinity Lutheran, Jefferson City.*

1875, who tended not only his flock at Zion but also the congregation of St. John's Lutheran Church in the small community of Schubert (at the time called Liberty) near Taos. Zion records indicate the yearly salary the two congregations provided in support of Pastor Wesche amounted to $250 in 1875. Trinity Lutheran in Jefferson City and Immanuel Lutheran Church in Honey Creek had, by this time, grown to the extent that they were able to call their own pastors rather than relying on the support of Zion Lutheran Church.

Palmer Scheperle, a descendant of some of the charter members of Zion Lutheran church, writes, "[Pastor Wesche] served for twelve years, during which time Zion saw that the congregation had outgrown the little log church, so work began on a more spacious structure. This brick building was finished in 1879 with furnishing made by local craftsmen. It served as a place of worship and also as school room." Scheperle's records go to note that this "church building served the congregation until 1906, when the present [brick] structure was built." He goes on to explain that "much of the old building was recycled and used in the new church, notably the balcony."

There were other pastors who served the congregation at Zion after Pastor Wesche's departure, but it was after his tenure, in 1889, that the decision was made at Zion that the pastor would be dedicated to their congregation, no longer working in support with Trinity Lutheran Church in Jefferson City or other congregations. Growth was a welcomed circumstance in the congregation and inspired discussions about the construction of a new church around the beginning of the twentieth century.

Records written by Palmer Scheperle indicate that Zion's first church building provided a house of worship to the new German immigrants for thirty-four years and the second structure stood for three decades. When discussions began about erecting the third (and current) church structure, many descendants of founding members were involved, such as Emil Fischer, who was appointed as chairman of the building committee along with fellow committee members Benjamin Loesch, Robert Loesch, Andrew Nieghorn and William Fischer.

The second church held a sad memory for one building committee member, Andrew Nieghorn, and his wife, Eva Heisinger. On October 11, 1894, thirteen-year-old Heinrich "Henry" Nieghorn fell from the narrow balcony inside Zion Lutheran Church, possibly while engaged in horseplay with other church youth. The fall caused what was cited as a hemorrhage and resulted in the death of the youth, who was then interred in the church cemetery. Years later, Heinrich's nephew, whom he never met, Ernest Nieghorn, would come of age while attending the same church and serve the congregation for decades as an organist.

Embracing the well-known German characteristics of working smartly while embracing efficiency, the congregation set up a sawmill on the property, and once the old church was leveled, many of the materials were repurposed for use in the third church building, which was dedicated in 1906. As noted on the church's registration form for the National Register of Historic Places, a distinguished list on which the church was placed in 2000, the third church building has changed very little in the past century. The registration noted of the Zion Church, "The brick building sits on a limestone foundation and measures approximately 28' x 50'." The report goes on to further describe the church as "an example of the Late Victorian Gothic Revival modified by vernacular Missouri German characteristics." Additionally, a large three-story tower became the central feature in the front of the church, the first floor of which served as an entrance. A stairway led to the second story, where congregation members could access the balcony from which to participate in worship services. On the third floor of the tower was an open belfry that housed the bell used to signal to the community the beginning of worship.

Opposite: The third and final structure to be used as Zion Lutheran Church was dedicated in 1906. *St. John's Lutheran, Stringtown.*

Right: The cornerstone of Zion Lutheran Church is inscribed in German, reading, "Built in 1906, thank the Lord." *Jeremy P. Ämick.*

A booklet printed in celebration of the 150th anniversary of Immanuel Lutheran Church in Honey Creek explains that shortly after the new church was finished in 1906, a schoolhouse was built. "This parochial school stood at the entrance of the cemetery where the second church had once been located."

Pastor W. Berndt was installed in 1908, at a time when the new church building had barely had the opportunity to settle on its limestone foundation. His tenure at Zion was brief, lasting only two years. However, during this time, coming on the heels of the major construction project of a new church building, the congregation came together to erect a new parsonage. This expansive home, which remains on the property, is two stories in height and was built with eight rooms.

The schoolhouse for the church was once located in the middle of the cemetery, where the second church building had once stood and near the current cemetery sign. According to the writings of Palmer Scheperle, the schoolhouse was destroyed in the late 1980s. Some church records indicate that the Christian Day School had been organized at Zion as early as 1865 and survived into the 1940s, at which time the congregation could no longer maintain a full-time pastor to serve as a teacher, nor could they compete with larger schools because of consolidation of districts.

The parish hall was constructed in the early 1940s and remains in useable condition on the church property. Like many parish halls, it provided a comfortable building where the church could hold its voters meetings, Sunday school classes, church dinners, wedding receptions and an assortment of other events. The spacious facility measures fifty feet in length and is thirty feet wide with a full basement.

As noted earlier, in the 1940s, facing the dilemma of declining student enrollment because of continued consolidation of local school districts and the difficulty in providing for teachers, the parochial school at Zion closed its doors. The same challenge of attendance would come to impact the church body as well. Eventually, a declining congregation and a lack of resources to support a full-time pastor inspired the decision for Zion to enter into a dual-parish arrangement with St. John's Lutheran Church in Stringtown.

"The last resident pastor at Zion was Rev. R.J. Oetjen, who served the church for a short time in 1946," explains Immanuel Lutheran Church's historical booklet.

Pastor Ernest Albert Bieberdorf, who was installed in 1948, became the first to serve both congregations under the dual-parish arrangement, although his full-time responsibilities were at St. John's Lutheran Church in Stringtown. He continued serving in this capacity for the next six years.

The communion window behind the altar at Zion Lutheran Church features the German phrase, "Das ist mein Leib, Das ist mein Blut" (this is my body, this is my blood). *Jeremy P. Ämick.*

Candace Stockton explained, "I grew up in that church [at Zion] and spent the first twenty years of my life there while my father, Ernest Loesch, was very active and served as president of the congregation; my mother was involved with many church groups as well." She added, "I was actually confirmed at St. John's [in Stringtown] by Pastor Bieberdorf, along with two other girls, because we didn't have a full-time pastor at Zion at that time."

"From 1946–1975, the pastor vacancy was filled by alternate ministers of other Lutheran congregations," the aforementioned booklet from Immanuel Lutheran Church explains. "The last pastor to conduct services at Zion was Rev. Arnold Griesse."

A combination of factors—such as the remote location of the church, an aging congregation, youth leaving the area and difficulties retaining a consistent pastor—resulted in waning membership at Zion Lutheran Church. The decision was eventually made to close the historic parish that had been a beacon of Christian hope for many generations of Lutheran families.

Pastor Hansen, who led the congregation of Zion on its one hundredth anniversary celebration in 1943, wrote of his hope for the future: "As we review the history of Zion, we meet with many evidences of God's blessing, chief among which is that He through all these years preserved His Holy Word and blessed Sacraments in her midst." His optimistic pen continued to write, "As Zion enters the second century of its existence, may she lift up her heart to God for the many blessing of the past and in the prayer that He continue to abide with her in His Word, His love and His gracious protection."

Yet as the instruction of "thy will be done," gifted to humanity through the Lord's Prayer, might imply, there were grander developments to come for Lutheranism in Cole County. This plan, though sadly resulting the loss of the Mother Church, came with the unexpected blessing of growth in nearby Lutheran congregations better situated in communities prepared to develop and embrace growth in membership in the coming years.

"I was always told by members of my family that the decline of [Zion Lutheran Church] was because it was located so close to Jefferson City and that many of the members began going to Trinity Lutheran while others migrated to St. John's in Stringtown," said Shawn Ehrhardt, who holds the distinction of being the last person baptized at Zion.

The final worship service was held at Zion Lutheran Church on October 26, 1975, and the congregation officially disbanded less than two years later, on July 3, 1977. With the closure of the church, many families, concerned about maintaining in perpetuity the final resting places of their family members and other loved ones, devised a plan to ensure the church cemetery did not become overgrown with weeds, a broken reminder of a once-glorious past.

"My late father, Alfred Ehrhardt, along with my uncle, Herman Hansen, and another church member, Harold Fischer, were among the trustees responsible for selling off the church property," explained Shawn Ehrhardt. "They sold everything except the cemetery, which they tried to run for a few years. I remember them meeting at our house in the early 1980s to discuss the disposition of the cemetery. That's when they decided to place it in a trust with a local bank, using the money from the earlier property sale

The two-story parsonage at Zion Lutheran Church was erected in 1908 and is now a private residence. *Jeremy P. Ämick.*

The parish hall at Zion was constructed in the early 1940s, predominantly through the labor of members of the congregation. *Jeremy P. Ämick.*

to help finance the cemetery's perpetual care." Solemnly, he added, "They knew they weren't getting any younger and needed to ensure the cemetery was cared for in the years to come."

For about five years after its closure, the church was leased to a Baptist congregation, who named it Mt. Zion Baptist Church. Then, for about seven years, the church building was converted into an antique store. In 2001, it was purchased by June Nivens, who has sought to maintain the character of the original church and even had a new altar built since the original was moved years earlier to St. John's Lutheran Church in Stringtown, where it is still in use. After the altar was moved to St. John's, the painting of Jesus was removed and framed; it now hangs on a wall inside the original front entrance of St. John's. There was a painting in the old altar used at St. John's that featured Jesus rescuing Peter from the raging seas, which was removed and installed in the altar from Zion. Several inches had to be cut from the top of the Zion altar for it to fit in the altar opening at St. John's. Regardless, the altar has been well cared for throughout the decades and continues to be used as a focal point during worship services.

Clarence Loesch and Anna Heil were married at Zion on April 27, 1963. In the background is the altar that was given to St. John's Lutheran Church in Stringtown after Zion closed. *Bill Loesch.*

Rev. Ernest Biberdorf was pastor of St. John's Lutheran Church for six years beginning in 1948. During this time, he also served as pastor of Zion through a dual-parish arrangement. *St. John's, Stringtown.*

The former church, now called the Zion Historic Chapel, is listed on the National Historic Registry and, though privately owned, can be rented for special events such as weddings and vow renewals. Also, a few years after the church was closed, the bell was removed from the belfry and has since been installed at United Methodist Church in Russellville. After purchasing the property, Nivens found another bell sitting in a wooded area a short distance behind the church, and it has been installed in the belfry. The parish hall has been maintained and, for the last several years, has been used for meetings by Shiloh, a local recovery group.

Aleda Renken, in an article printed in the October 9, 1975 edition of the *Daily Capital News*, poignantly remarked that the primary characteristic that made Zion Lutheran Church such a special place remained even after its closure—the recollections of those who gathered there for worship.

"But you can't sell a church, you can only sell a building. The church will stay alive in the memories of those who were confirmed there, those who were married there and those who grew old there."

CHRISTOPHER ARNHOLD: CHARTER MEMBER OF ZION AND PIONEER GERMAN IMMIGRANT OF BRAZITO AREA

The Arnhold name was once synonymous with the Brazito community. It represented an immigrant who settled in Cole County and not only helped establish the mother of all Lutheran churches in the area but also worked to found a successful mercantile business. Years later, his son took over the business and assumed an active role in the founding of yet another church in the rural area of the county.

Christopher Arnhold was born in Prussia on April 9, 1814, and, in his early years, trained as a carpenter. He immigrated to the United States in 1842, settling in St. Louis prior to making the journey to Jefferson City along the Missouri River. Family historical records indicate that he came from a family who had gained experience owning and operating mills in Germany, which provided a real-world education that would be beneficial in his later commercial endeavors.

"In 1843 he came to Jefferson City, where he was married to Miss Pauline, a daughter of Gotleib Frisch, by whom he became the father of four children," explains the *Godspeed's History of Cole County* printed in 1889.

Marriage was not the only high point in Arnhold's life in 1843; that year, he also partnered with several of his fellow immigrants in founding Zion Lutheran Church south of Jefferson City. This church would go on to help plant Lutheran congregations in Lohman, Stringtown, Honey Creek and Jefferson City.

Arnhold's twenty-nine-year-old wife passed away in 1852 and was laid to rest in what later became the Trinity Lutheran Cemetery in Jefferson City. He later married Elizabeth Werkmann, with whom he raised four children.

In the booklet *Cole County Cooking and Culture*, which was printed in honor of the nation's bicentennial in 1976, it is written that Christopher Arnhold departed his Jefferson City home and became "the man credited with founding Brazito, in or about 1854."

The community assumed its name from a soldier who served in 1846 during the Battle of El Brazito in the Mexican-American War and who later settled in Cole County. History has somehow managed to conceal the identity of this soldier, although some records indicate he might have been William Crede.

In the years prior to the Civil War, Arnhold lived in Camden County and established Arnhold's Mill, once located a few miles west of Linn Creek on the Niangua River, not far from the springs of Ha Ha Tonka. During the Civil War, the Arnhold family had to flee to the safety of a nearby farm after they were driven from their home one evening by suspected bushwhackers. They were shocked to later discover that while the mayhem of the moment unfolded, their home, storehouse and gristmill had burned to the ground. The location where the mill and homestead once stood has been underwater since the early 1930s following the construction of Bagnell Dam and the Lake of the Ozarks.

The aforementioned booklet notes Arnhold's return to Cole County and his ownership of "extensive amounts of land in the business area of Brazito. He began a general store in 1872. The only other business at that time was a harness shop."

The Arnhold Store was a nucleus of activity for the Brazito area and was established near the site of what is now a convenience store and gas station.

Christopher Arnhold was a founding member of Zion Lutheran Church. Years later, he helped establish Brazito and opened the Arnhold General Store. *Friedens Church Brazito.*

Christopher Arnhold's son from his second marriage, Charles A. Arnhold, purchased one-half interest in the store in 1880 and assumed full ownership of the business five years later.

On his death at seventy-seven years of age in 1891, the newspaper described Arnhold as "one of the oldest and highly respected citizens of the county." He was laid to rest in a family plot he established in Brazito called the Arnhold Burial Ground.

Wilhelm Martin Mohr: Charter Member of Zion and Half-Brother of "Silent Night" Author

The holy refrain of "Silent Night" has long been incorporated into Christmas celebrations worldwide. Written by Father Joseph Mohr, a Catholic priest and Austrian native, the song is still sung in its original German by some local churches on Christmas Eve. The words of Father Mohr are interestingly woven into the fabric of a forgotten Lutheran church near Jefferson City, where the half brother of the song's writer became a founding member of the congregation after immigrating to Missouri.

"In the year of 1792, Anna Schoiberen was a seamstress in Salzburg, Austria, and she had no one to sponsor her infant son Joseph for baptism [since] the father, Franz Joseph Mohr, a soldier who boarded in the home, had abandoned her," writes the late Palmer Scheperle, a descendant of the Mohr family. "Franz Joseph Mohr not only fled from the home but also deserted the Austrian army. He reappeared in Salzburg after nineteen years, in 1811, the same year Wilhelm [Martin] Mohr was born. History does not tell us where he spent the nineteen years."

Although Wilhelm Mohr carried the surname of the soldier who fathered his older brother, the actual identity of his father is not known; however, he was one of four illegitimate children born to his unmarried mother.

In 1818, when Wilhelm Mohr was seven years old, his older brother, Catholic priest Joseph Mohr, penned the words to "Silent Night" and asked his friend Franz Gruber to compose music for it on the guitar. That Christmas Eve, the song was performed for the first time in Father Mohr's church.

It is doubtful that Joseph Mohr had much of a relationship with his younger half brother, since he was already in seminary at the time of Wilhelm's birth. One certainty is that young Wilhelm was raised in poverty prior to somehow finding the resources to leave his homeland.

Father Joseph Mohr wrote the lyrics for "Silent Night," a popular Christmas song. His half-brother, Wilhelm, immigrated to Missouri and was a founding member of Zion Lutheran Church. *Jeremy P. Ämick.*

Scheperle explains that Wilhelm "immigrated to America in about 1840 and settled in Cole County, near Jefferson City in the Zion Community, and homesteaded eighty acres adjacent and east of the present-day Jefferson City Country Club on South Country Club Drive."

After coming to America, Wilhelm began using "William" as his first name. Scheperle speculates that he would have been Catholic, just as his older brother, but later converted to Lutheranism. Immigration records indicate Wilhelm departed from Hesse-Darmstadt in Germany, a region bordering Lower Saxony. His movement to the United States parallels a period defined by the mass migration of Lutherans to the area.

"One of the bands united for emigration by the same motives and purposes were the Saxon immigrants who came to Missouri during January and February of 1839," writes Professor Theodore Buenges in the book *Ebenezer: Reviews of the Work of the Missouri Synod during Three Quarters of a Century*. Buenges adds, "With two later additions that comprise a total of not quite 1,000 persons. These 1,000 immigrants must be considered the most important group among the 68,069 new arrivals of that year, and their settlement one of very much consequence for the country."

The year 1843 heralded a period of new beginnings for the thirty-two-year-old Wilhelm Mohr as he married Anna Katherina Wolf on May 2, 1843, and, a little more than two months later, became one of thirty-seven charter members who formed Zion Lutheran Church a few miles south of Jefferson City.

His wife's parents, Christoph and Anna (Vogel) Wolf, were also recent immigrants to Missouri from Germany and settled in the community located in proximity to Zion Lutheran Church, the first Lutheran church in the county. Additionally, Christoph Wolf was listed alongside his new son-in-law as a founding member of Zion. Throughout the next several years, Mohr and his wife raised nine children and toiled to eke out a living on their farm, all while remaining dedicated to their Lutheran faith.

Scheperle explains that the seventy-eight-year-old Wilhelm Mohr, no stranger to hard work, "died suddenly on July 6, 1889 on his farm that he homesteaded in April of 1840, while he and his neighbors were harvesting his wheat crop."

Wilhelm's wife passed away twenty years later and lies alongside him in the cemetery of Zion Lutheran Church. Wilhelm's older brother, Father Joseph Mohr, died in a village near Salzburg, Austria, on December 4, 1848 when only fifty-five years old. "Stille Nacht," or "Silent Night," as it is known in English, became a favorite tune of King Friedrich Wilhelm IV of Prussia and earned Mohr worldwide fame after his death.

Wilhelm Mohr came to learn that the song was attributed to his half brother as immigrants from Saxony and surrounding regions continued settling in Missouri, sharing the beloved melody at churches in the area. For many years, Wilhelm would sing the sweet refrain in German on Christmas Eve among his fellow congregation members at Zion.

Zion Lutheran Church held its final worship service in 1975. However, Wilhelm Mohr's legacy carries on through congregations like St. John's Lutheran Church in Stringtown, which was established through the loving work of Zion and where "Stille Nacht" continues to be sung on Christmas Eve.

Wilhelm Mohr and his wife are interred in the cemetery of Zion Lutheran Church. *Jeremy P. Ämick.*

In the insightful words of famed American statesman Benjamin Franklin, "If you would not be forgotten as soon as you are dead, either write something worth reading or do something worth writing."

The Mohr brothers accomplished both. Though living a world apart in adulthood, they have through their work imparted a lasting legacy— Wilhelm by helping founded a church that resulted in the establishment of many other congregations still active in the local community and his half brother, Joseph, a Catholic priest, by crafting the lyrics to a beautiful song that is still embraced throughout the world.

ERNEST NIEGHORN: LONGTIME ORGANIST FOR ZION LUTHERAN CHURCH

The late Ernest "Ernie" Nieghorn lived a story that is a blend of tragedy, interesting historical moments and service to others. A descendant of an early immigrant family, he was not averse to hard work, adored music, enjoyed reading the comforting words of the Bible and, despite experiencing the loss of his loved ones, helped provide for the future education of Lutheran youth in the Stringtown area.

Born in Cole County in 1915, Ernie Nieghorn was raised on a small farm near the intersections of Route CC and US Highway 54 south of Jefferson City. A small creek running through the property, the Nieghorn Branch, was named for his great-grandfather Johann, a German immigrant who became an early member of Zion Lutheran Church.

"The Zion public school closed Friday, with one graduate, Ernest Nieghorn," reported the *Jefferson City News Tribune* on May 3, 1929.

Although completion of the eighth grade represented the termination of Nieghorn's formal education, he read voraciously and learned to play the piano and organ. As the years passed, he worked on his father's farm and gained a reputation as a capable pitcher while playing for several local baseball teams.

"I had heard that there was a professional baseball team that was scouting him at one point during his playing days," said Don Buchta, a local historian. "For some reason, he never decided to pursue it."

The year 1940 ushered in the first moment of misfortune for young Nieghorn when his mother, Eleonora, passed away from liver cancer when only forty-nine years old. She was laid to rest in the cemetery of Zion Lutheran Church.

Ernie Nieghorn was a member of Zion Lutheran Church and was known for the animated manner in which he played the organ during church services. *St. John's Lutheran, Stringtown.*

Then came World War II, the beginning of a defining time in Nieghorn's life. His younger brother, Gilbert, was inducted into the U.S. Army Air Corps early in the war and was reported missing after the fall of Corregidor in May 1942. The following month, Ernie was inducted into the U.S. Army and went on to train as an infantryman.

For the next year, Nieghorn embarked on his own cycle of military training, uncertain whether his brother was still alive. Sadly, in April 1943, Gilbert's status was changed from "missing in action" to "casualty."

"Pvt. Ernest C. Nieghorn…has returned to Camp Rucker, Ala., after spending a 10-day furlough here," reported the *Sunday News and Tribune* on December 27, 1942.

Nieghorn was assigned to the 322nd Infantry Regiment, which was organized at Camp Rucker less than two weeks after his induction. According to the book *World War II Order of Battle*, the regiment was under the 81st Division and conducted maneuvers in Tennessee prior to moving to California for additional training and overseas deployment.

The regiment departed San Francisco in June 1944 and arrived Guadalcanal several weeks later. In September 1944, they participated in the assault on Anguar Island before moving on to Peleliu and New Caledonia. The latter location was where Nieghorn's service came to a close.

"He told me that while he was in the service, he volunteered to play a portable organ for the chaplains during religious services," said Rev. Warren Brandt, who came to know Nieghorn in later years. "Also, I recall him telling me that he was pulled off the front lines for awhile after he contracted some type of illness due to the unsanitary conditions."

According to his separation papers, Private First Class Nieghorn was sent back to the States and released from the army at the Hospital Center at Camp Carson, Colorado, on May 28, 1945. At the time, his regiment was still stationed in the Philippines. Returning to the Jefferson City area, Nieghorn purchased his father's property in 1946. His younger sister, Lydia, had been placed in an assisted living facility after the passing of their mother years earlier since she required dedicated care because of a mental illness.

"He was a great musician and had a fun, silly personality," said Candace Stockton, a longtime member of Zion Lutheran Church. "He knew the Bible better than most ministers and taught very interesting Bible classes." Stockton continued, "He was the organist at Zion and was known for taking off his shoes to play the organ in his socks because he didn't want to get the foot pedals dirty. He was exceptionally talented and quite lively when he played music."

For many years, Nieghorn worked for Arthur W. Ellis, Inc., a tire supply and repair company in Jefferson City that later became Ewers Tires, Inc. In the late 1970s, when the congregation of Zion Lutheran Church disbanded, Nieghorn transferred his membership to St. John's Lutheran Church in Stringown.

Nieghorn was inducted into the U.S. Army in June 1942, at a time when his younger brother, Gilbert, was missing in action in the South Pacific. *St. John's Lutheran, Stringtown.*

"I came to St. John's as pastor in 1985 and Ernie [Nieghorn] was already retired," said Rev. Warren Brandt. "He had a special place in his heart for the children and would always have a sack of candy to hand out to them after church services." Grinning, Brandt added, "I remember he filled in for the organist during one of our Reformation services and told me to be ready, because he was going to play the song 'A Mighty Fortress' and really 'open it up until the roof came off the place.'"

On December 29, 1987, the seventy-two-year-old Nieghorn passed away and was laid to rest in Zion Lutheran Cemetery, where generations of his family had attended services. His estate was left to the congregation of St. John's Lutheran Church in Stringtown and has provided resources and materials for the youth of the congregation.

"He never married or had any children of his own, but he has left quite a legacy and wanted to make sure the children in the congregation received a good Christian education," said Brandt.

In the fellowship hall at St. John's Lutheran Church, there hangs on the wall a handcrafted remembrance box containing the U.S. flag that draped Nieghorn's coffin, his military photograph and his brother's Purple Heart medal.

"Ernie was always smiling, friendly, told great stories and was well read," said Rev. Brandt. "If you met him, you would never forget him."

CHAPTER 2

ST. JOHN'S LUTHERAN CHURCH

(SCHUBERT)

*From Frontier Preaching Station
to an Enduring Lutheran Legacy*

St. John's Lutheran Church in the community of Schubert near Taos has a verifiable history dating back to 1844, in essence making it the second Lutheran congregation to come to Cole County, just after Zion Lutheran Church. It was during this year that a group of Bavarian immigrants (followed by Austrians and Swabians), having recently settled in the area, purchased sections of property a half mile east of the present church. They soon banded together to organize the Osage Point Church.

"Schubert was once quite a bustling community," said Pastor Gerald Scheperle, who has been pastor at St. John's Lutheran Church in Schubert since 1980 and is now the longest-serving in the congregation's history. "There used to be several businesses like a tavern, blacksmith shop, hatchery and dancehall, all of which have disappeared."

The Osage Point Church, although established as a Lutheran congregation, was in its early years often supported by pastors from Zion Lutheran Church south of Jefferson City in addition to missionary pastors traveling through the area. These pastors from the Missouri Synod or the Iowa Synod, German Evangelicals or "anyone who could stop by and preach," Scheperle said.

The beginnings of St. John's Lutheran Church unfolded on December 5, 1866, when Lorenz Schubert, George Schuster and Albert Koehler—trustees for Osage Point Church—purchased the 4.45-acre property a short distance to the west, where the church is now located. Historical records reveal that this property was intially purchased in 1850 for the purpose of establishing a Methodist Episcopal church, which never came to fruition.

Organized as Osage Point Church in 1844, St. John's Lutheran Church moved to its current location in Schubert after the Civil War. *Jeremy P. Ämick.*

"Osage Point had really just been a preaching station, and we believe it consisted of a log church that is no longer there," Scheperle explained. "The old church may have been disassembled and moved here to use as the first church for St. John's. There is also a small cemetery off Lisletown Road near where the Osage Point Church was once located. When they purchased the current property we are on now, it was so that they could be situated closer to the Old St. Louis Road that later became US Highway 50."

Church documents indicate that in 1868, Pastor Conrad Duerschner, who was at the time serving a call to St. Paul's Lutheran Church in Lohman, which was part of the Iowa Synod, began providing pastoral support to the budding congregation in Schubert. Around this time, a small parsonage was built, and in 1869, St. John's Lutheran Church officially organized as a congregation.

For the next fifty years, St. John's was predominantly supported by pastors affiliated with the Iowa Synod. The congregation's first resident pastor was Rudolf Pfister, who remained with the church until 1870. During his brief time with the Schubert congregation, a small log church was erected. Next came Pastor Christoph Schober, who remained for five years until being succeeded by Pastor H. Wesche, who remained until 1878. His replacement was Pastor Robert Falke, a recent seminary graduate who remained for three years.

Pastor Conrad Mutschmann-Gebert, a German native and graduate of Wartburg Seminary, was "installed at St. John's late in 1881 and tended the flock here until he died of heart disease June 2, 1885 at age 33," as a historical bulletin describes. "Pastor Mutschmann is buried in our cemetery along with two of his infant children that died the day after birth." The bulletin adds, "It is known…that during his pastorate an organ was purchased from a New Jersey firm for St. John's Church."

Rev. Robert L. Falke was installed as pastor at St. John's Lutheran Church in 1878, remaining with the congregation for three years. *St. John's Lutheran, Schubert.*

The next pastoral call was submitted to Ernest Frederick Geyer, another recent seminary graduate still residing in Germany. His pastorate, beginning in 1886, was an exciting period accompanied by the construction of a new church and parsonage.

"In the early months of 1889 it was decided that the continued growth of the congregation necessitated the erection of a new church building," notes the one hundredth anniversary booklet printed by the members of St. John's in 1969. "The weather-boarded building that had served the parish since c. 1870…had become too small."

Designed by Jefferson City architect William Vogdt, the Gothic-style brick church, which continues to serve the congregation, was built at the cost of $4,900. In 1897, a new parsonage was also built, and the old church building was used for several years as a parochial school.

The Lutheran congregation at the former Emanuel Lutheran Church in Centertown, which is highlighted in a later chapter, entered into a dual-parish agreement during Pastor Geyer's tenure at Schubert. This agreement remained in effect for several years; however, the church in Centertown began its decline in membership in the 1920s, and all that remains is an empty lot flanked by a cemetery. Pastor Geyer remained with St. John's until 1902, at the time having earned the distinction of being the longest-serving pastor for the congregation. (His detailed story is shared in the subsequent

In 1889, it was decided to build a new brick church for the congregation of St. John's. In 1897, a new parsonage was also built, and the old church building was used for several years as a parochial school. *St. John's Lutheran, Schubert.*

pages.) The next several years brought many changes as several pastors filled the pulpit, but in 1921, the church welcomed Rev. Otto Bernthal and made the official transition to the Missouri Synod.

Additions and improvements have been made to the church and surrounding property in recent years. Several pastors have come and gone, but all since 1942 have supported the dual-parish arrangement that continues between St. John's in Schubert and St. John's Evangelical Lutheran Church in Babbtown. Pastor Scheperle, who has served both these Lutheran congregations for more than four decades, notes that the church in Schubert holds a special distinction among other Lutheran congregations in Cole County.

"We are one of the oldest Lutheran churches in the county, and Zion, which was the oldest, is now closed," he said. "Our church has been continuously sharing the Gospel since 1844, and that's an achievement worthy of celebration." Scheperle added, "St. John's in Schubert has vacillated between different synods throughout the decades, but the need for a pastor and a solid Gospel-centered ministry became an important part of our history. We were a small church, and both Iowa and Missouri Synods wanted to lay their claim on the congregation, but history has a way of unfolding in unexpected ways. Fortunately, our church remains a strong anchor in a bygone community."

Pastor William W. Ferren, who served the congregation at St. John's in Schubert from 1967 until 1974, wrote of his beloved church in 1969, "In reviewing the history of St. John's, from the humble beginnings of the Osage Point Church to today, we too are moved to cry out, 'The Lord has done great things for us; we are glad!' (Psalms 115:1) What is chronicled…is not the record of human achievement but testimony to the blessings of Almighty God. It is truly 'A Century of Grace in a County Place' and more."

REV. ERNST FRIEDRICH GEYER: GERMAN-BORN PASTOR WHO LED LUTHERAN FAITHFUL IN COLE COUNTY

Ernst Friedrich Geyer was born near Greiz, Germany, on April 19, 1865, and baptized in the Chrisitan faith several days later. He was at a young age exposed to a life of service to others since his father was administrator for a home that cared for neglected children. This experience inspired Ernst's decision to enter the ministry and immigrate to Missouri, where he met his wife in Lohman and supported congregations in Schubert and Centertown.

Confirmed on Palm Sunday in 1879, years later, Geyer attended four years of seminary in Neuendettelsau, Germany, from where he graduated in 1886. He then departed his homeland and family to embark on a career in the ministry in an area of the United States teeming with German immigrants. An anniversary booklet from St. John's Lutheran Church in Schubert explains that Pastor Geyer "was called by St. John's while still in his native Germany. He accepted the call and was ordained and installed here in 1886."

Shortly after his arrival in Missouri, Geyer met many of the Lutheran families living in Lohman. This included a young womany named Anna Blochberger, to whom he was soon engaged. On January 24, 1888, in a ceremony at St. Paul's Lutheran Church in Lohman, they were married by Pastor George Fikenscher, a fellow German native who was at the time serving as St. Paul's pastor. The couple went on to have eleven children, ten of whom survived into adulthood. A number of these children were born while Geyer was serving the congregation in Schubert. In 1889, the year following his marriage, work began on erecting the new brick church that continues to serve members of St. John's.

It was also during Geyer's tenure at St. John's that a new parsonage was erected, providing the necessary lodging for his growing family. Although busy with family life, preparing sermons and calling on the sick and afflicted

In 1888, two years after being installed as pastor of St. John's Lutheran Church in Schubert, Ernst Geyer married Anna Blochberger of Lohman. *Gert Strobel.*

within the Schubert congregation, he chose to accept a call to a small and struggling Lutheran church on the opposite end of the county.

"At the January 1, [1891] meeting of St. John's voters, a delegation from Centertown appeared to ask that Pastor Geyer hold services there once a month since their pastor had taken a call elsewhere," note historical records maintained by St. John's. "After a lively and lengthy discussion, their request was granted, and St. John's became a dual-parish with Emanuel Church, Centertown [no longer in existence]. In 1893, Emanuel sent a regular call to Pastor Geyer, asking that he come to Centertown every three weeks....On the days that the pastor went to Emanuel, St. John's was to have afternoon services."

Pastor Geyer served at St. John's in Schubert for fourteen years before receiving a call to Nebraska, where he served two Lutheran churches prior to his death. *St. John's Lutheran, Schubert.*

Due to the small size of the Centertown congregation, they struggled for many years to accommodate a full-time pastor, not only relying on Pastor Geyer but also, on other occasions, being served by pastors from other congregations such as St. Paul's Lutheran Church in California. The dual-parish arrangement between St. John's and Centertown remained in place until 1897, at which time it was terminated over "dissatisfaction with afternoon services." Years later, this arrangement between St. John's and Emanuel in Centertown would be reinstated under a different pastorship.

During his tenure with St. John's, Pastor Geyer also strove to write a constitution for the church, but one was not accepted by the congregation while he remained with the church.

"Pastor Geyer accepted a call to Millard, Nebraska in May 1900, where he stayed until accepting a call to Long Branch, Nebraska in 1902," church records note.

For more than thirty years, Pastor Geyer faithfully served his church family in Long Branch and on the board of directors for the Iowa Synod, giving his last sermon in October 1933.

"This community was pained to learn of the death of Reverend E.F. Geyer, who if he had lived until July would have held the pastorate of Long Branch Church for some 32 years," reported Nebraska's *Humboldt Standard* on May 25, 1934.

The sixty-nine-year-old, having dedicated his entire adult life to the ministry, entered into the arms of his Lord on May 22, 1934. His body was laid to rest in the cemetery of St. James Lutheran Church in Nemaha County, Nebraska, where in years previous he had preached innumerable sermons.

"Anna Marjorie Geyer, a resident of this community, died very suddenly… [on] November 3, 1943, at the home of her daughter, Mrs. George Burow," the *Humboldt Standard* noted the day following her death. "Mr. Geyer, who was a minister, passed away in 1934. Since his death, Mrs. Geyer has made her home with her children."

Newspapers often provide a simple recounting of facts, but on the passing of Rev. Geyer, the longtime servant of three Lutheran congregations in two neighboring states, they lavished him with admiration for his stalwart work in the ministry.

"He was a faithful servant of his Master and tried to bring souls of his congregation to Christ the Savior, and his services were never tiring," wrote the *Humboldt Standard* on June 1, 1934. "He was loved by many and his home was always open for visitors and lending a helping hand to all. Although he was afflicted with many ailments the last few years, he clung to his Lord and Savior whom he had served so many years."

JACOB SCHMUTZLER: GERMAN IMMIGRANT WHO ESTABLISHED A FARM NEAR SCHUBERT COMMUNITY

In 1872, a nineteen-year-old Jacob Schmutzler emigrated from the recently unified German Empire following the Franco-Prussian War, eventually settling in Cole County. He later met and married Mary Goser and, in 1889, purchased a farm that has since earned the impressive name of Missouri Century Farm, providing both a home and livelihood for several generations of the Schmutzler family.

"The general warranty deed states that my grandfather, Jacob Schmutzler, purchased the farm from M.B. and Nancy Taylor in 1889," said Ronda Williams.

Williams's brother, Mark Schmutzler, noted that the farm sprawled across 164 acres and was located along Big Meadows Road about a quarter mile west of the Osage River and a couple miles east of Taos.

Jacob Schmutzler and his wife became parents to five children, four of whom lived into adulthood. Having carried with them from Germany their Lutheran faith, Schmutzler and his family were members of St. John's Lutheran Church in the nearby community of Schubert, where the children attended the parish-sponsored school. Jacob imbued his only son, John, with an interest in agriculture while toiling on their farm, work that consisted predominantly of sowing and harvesting grain in addition to raising cattle. When Jacob passed away in 1900 and was laid to rest in the cemetery of St. John's Lutheran Church, John took over the farm and was later assisted by Elizabeth Dippold, whom he married in 1914. He erected barns on the farm in 1914 and 1918, both of which still stand.

The Schmutzler Farm was established by Jacob Schmutzler in 1889. Pictured is his only son, John Schmutzler, who married Elizabeth Dippold in 1914. *The Schmutzler family.*

"Unfortunately, I do not remember much about my father, because he died on September 17, 1940, when I was seven years old," recalled Lois Gershefske, youngest of the six children born to John and Elizabeth Schmutzler. "His passing left my mother to raise two young girls, because my other siblings were several years older." Pausing, she continued, "This was a very challenging time for my mother, and if it had not been for the help of my older brothers and sisters, it would have been nearly impossible for her."

The first home built on the farm was a log structure, which was later replaced by a wood-frame house. Gershefske recalled that when she was a child, her family learned to survive in the absence of running water, electricity and indoor restrooms, while all of their heating and cooking was accomplished with woodburning stoves. She also explained that her older brothers, Clarence and Adolph Schmutzler, assisted with the farm duties following the death of their father. However, when Adolph was drafted into the U.S. Army during World War II, Clarence was shorthanded and leaned on his siblings for assistance.

"That is when we gals (Anna Marie, Emily and I) became 'milk maids' to help out," Lois Gershefske wrote in a brief family history. "We had dairy cows and sold milk, and those cows had to be milked twice a day, every day of the week." In reflection, she added, "Tractors took the place of horses sometime during this period but there weren't any combines. My older sister, Anna Marie, rode on top of the binder that was pulled behind a tractor and operated all of the levers that made it function."

When Adolph returned from the war, he found employment in Jefferson City and also worked on the farm but later married and moved to Holts Summit. Clarence went on to become a carpenter and also served as an insurance appraiser. Clarence married Leona Heidbreder in 1948, and the couple eventually settled on the Schmutzler Farm. A brick house was built on the property in 1969 and is still used as a residence. Clarence and Leona raised three children: Mark, Ronda and Dale. The family entered its fourth generation of ownership when Dale took over farm operations in the years following his father's death in 1980.

"I graduated with a degree in agricultural engineering from the University of Missouri in 1982 and was employed with SEMA [State Emergency Management Agency] from 1983–2020, working on the farm in my spare time," Dale Schmutzler said. "I have many great memories of growing up around here," he added. "But I think that one of the more interesting features of the property is the little cemetery in the middle of one of the fields where many of the Taylors are buried, which is the family my great-grandfather purchased the farm from."

There is an old two-seat carriage that was used by their great-grandfather but had been stored for many years in a machine shed on the farm. Despite its rough condition, it was restored by Gerald Scheperle, pastor of St. John's Lutheran Church in Schubert, and displayed during activities in 2019 celebrating the 175th anniversary of church's founding.

The father of two sons, Ross and Ethan, Dale Schmutzler finds comfort knowing the farm tradition established by his great-grandfather in the nineteenth century will continue to provide pleasant remembrances for future generations of his family. His aunt, Lois Gershefske, explained that visiting her childhood home continues to stir up many delightful memories.

"A lot of people talk about growing up under dreadful circumstances, but I was certainly blessed to have been raised in a God-fearing family with strong values and a great work ethic," she said. "I have been blessed from day one—and that's not to say that we didn't have difficult times. We may have been financially poor, but our parents made sure we had food on the table, and we got by just fine. If times ever get tough again and we return to that kind of situation, we know that we can make it."

CHAPTER 3

ST. PAUL'S EVANGELICAL LUTHERAN
CHURCH (LOHMAN)

The Roots of Lutheranism Spread to the "Church on the Hill"

For several decades, Gert Strobel not only served as the organist for "the Church on the Hill in Lohman" and selflessly volunteered her free time on multiple church boards but also worked diligently to retain records of the history of the church, where several generations of her family had worshipped. Her detailed work has been supplemented by fellow church member and area historian Don Buchta, whose grandfather, John Jacob Buchta, helped establish Trinity Lutheran Church in Russellville, a sister congregation that is highlighted in chapter 10. These two individuals, along with several others since the founding of the church, have left a treasure trove of information regarding the formation and growth of the second Lutheran church in Cole County, St. Paul's Evangelical Lutheran Church in Lohman.

"It was the fortieth year of the past century [1840] that the first settlers came to this area," explains the historical booklet printed in 1952 on the occasion of the one hundredth anniversary of St. Paul's Lutheran Church. "Most of them were Bavarians. In the beginning of the [1850s] they were joined by Austrians and Swabians because of a distinctive movement of the people in Bavaria and Oberfranke at that time. Just a very few came here. Those that came found a new home, but they did not find their church here."

Many eventually settled in the community that was initially platted as Stringtown, which, years later, had its name changed to Lohman after successful entrepreneur Charles W. Lohman established a post office and his store there in the early 1880s. Having brought with them from their ancestral

In 1852, John Paul Kalb, pastor of Zion Lutheran Church, assisted with the organization of St. Paul's Lutheran Church in Lohman. *Jeremy P. Ämick.*

homeland their Lutheran faith, these immigrants soon set about forming a church that continues to serve as a beacon to the surrounding community. Oftentimes, the decisions made by such migrants to settle in communities like Lohman was motivated by "uncertainties in their homeland," explains Charles Ravensway in *The Art and Architecture of German Settlements in Missouri*. These included disease, famine and revolution, while many of these immigrants were inspired by a "new country that held promise for higher income for the artisan and of cheaper land for the peasant."

"It was in the year 1852, that the desire to perpetuate the Lutheran faith brought together the heads of a number of emigrant families in the Stringtown area of west-central Cole County, Missouri," notes the *History of St. Paul's Church* published in 1977. "Residents of the area, since the previous decade, these transplanted Bavarians, Westphalians, Saxons and Austrians, dreamed of the establishment of a real church, one in which the catechism could be taught, marriages and burials celebrated in a traditional manner, and in which their firmly held belief in Grace and Justification would find expression."

These families found assistance in organizing this dream through Pastor John Paul Kalb, who was at the time serving as pastor of Zion Lutheran

Rev. Conrad Duerschner led the congregation at St. Paul's in Lohman from 1867 to 1871. *St. Paul's Lutheran, Lohman.*

Church near Jefferson City. At the time, Kalb was serving as a circuit pastor and providing spiritual guidance to several growing Lutheran congregations in the outlying rural areas. In 1852, Pastor Kalb met at the home of fifty-year-old John Adam Plochberger with Andrew Kautsch, John Nicol Koehler, John Jacob Ritter, John Schatz and John Schmidt to embark on the grand process of establishing a house of worship. The following year, on August 17, 1853, forty acres of land owned by John Jacob Kautsch, a founder of the new church, was sold for fifty dollars to John Plochberger and Andrew Kautsch (brother of John Jacob). Both John Plochberger and Andrew Kautsch were trustees for the "German Evangelical Lutheran Congregation unaltered Augsburg Confession named St. Paul Church," historical documents reveal.

Missionary pastors such as Pastor Kalb, who served multiple congregations spread over expansive rural areas, were a hardy and dedicated lot. They are described by Walter Baepler in *A Century of Grace* as "self-sacrificing men, whose hearts throbbed with the love of Christ and His people, whose religious convictions were sincere and deep, who were staunch and sturdy in all sorts of weather." Travel was accomplished on horseback and other times on foot, in weather conditions that were often less than favorable and through areas that were surrounded by thicket and forest, necessitating that a path be made in the absence of a discernible system of roads.

The new St. Paul's Evangelical Lutheran Church, like its "mother" congregation at nearby Zion, became part of the Missouri Synod, which had been formed only five years earlier. Shortly after the congregation of St. Paul's was established, Pastor Kalb left to accept a call to a congregation in Ohio and was replaced by Carl Wilhelm Frederking, who was installed as pastor on April 28, 1852, serving in that capacity for the next three years. Sometime during Pastor Frederking's tenure at St. Paul's, the hardscrabble parishioners worked together to erect the first church on the western slope of a hill overlooking the area that would years later become Lohman. The first church structure, history notes, was of simple log construction and provided a spiritual home to the congregation for nearly two decades.

Following the departure of Pastor Frederking in 1855, there was a brief vacancy until Zion Lutheran Church installed as its new pastor Emil Wege in 1856. As did his predecessors, Wege served several Lutheran congregations in the area, including St. Paul's. He remained in service to the congregation for the next ten years, providing spiritual guidance and emotional comfort through the difficult period of the Civil War, which was highlighted by two trying moments for the growing church. First, two of the congregation members—Friedrich Strobel and Erhardt Kautsch—died from their wounds after being shot by Confederate troops under the command of General Sterling Price near Stringtown on October 8, 1864. Both were buried in the church cemetery. Then, in the year following the end of the Civil War, St. Paul's history notes that Pastor Wege "caused serious dissatisfaction in the congregation which led to a complaint to the [Missouri] Synod. Since they got no hearing from the president of the Synod, the congregation separated itself from the [Missouri] Synod and joined the [Evangelical Lutheran] Synod of Iowa and Other States."

This controversy, which has been described as a doctrinal dispute, resulted in the decision of several founding members to break away from St. Paul's. In 1867, this group went on to organize St. John's Lutheran Church in nearby Stringtown and maintained their association with the Missouri Synod. A wide divergence of views within the Missouri Synod resulted in many former members leaving and organizing the Evangelical Lutheran Synod of Iowa in 1854. For many years, the two groups tried to meet in an attempt to resolve their differences in relation to their views on certain articles of faith, seeking to find a platform of unity; however, within a few years, it was realized this would not be achievable. At the time of the separation that occurred at St. Paul's shortly after the Civil War, Dr. C.F.W. Walther was serving as president of the Missouri Synod and had long been invested in reconciling the strife between the Iowa and Missouri Synods. Pastor Wege, who was at the time the pastor providing spiritual guidance to the congregation of St. Paul's, had years earlier immigrated to Missouri from Saxony with Dr. Walther and was a relatively close acquaintance of his. Essentially, what unfolded at St. Paul's in that tumultuous period appears to have been a subset of a greater issue that had been brewing between different Lutheran synods.

It was at the time of the split that the pastors of Zion Lutheran Church, a Missouri Synod congregation, discontinued their service to St. Paul's, as the Lohman congregation would now be supported by pastors associated with the Iowa Synod. The first of these was Pastor Joseph Meyer, who was installed in the spring of 1865 and the same year married Anna, a native of

The second church building of St. Paul's Lutheran Church was completed in 1872. It was replaced by a brick building dedicated in 1924. *Candace Stockton.*

Austria. Pastor Meyer left St. Paul's in 1867 to accept a call to a church in Iowa, and little is known about his life following this, although newspaper records indicate that he later accepted a pastorate with St. John's Lutheran Church in Fort Wayne, Indiana. His family experienced tragedy in 1905 when their eight-year-old daughter, Clara Anna, died from convulsions. Pastor Meyer passed away around the beginning of the twentieth century, and his wife later moved to Russellville, Missouri, where she lived for several years with her niece until she passed away in 1932. At the time of her death, she had a son, named for his father, Joseph Meyer, who was born while his parents were living in Lohman. The younger Meyer followed in his father's footsteps, becoming a Lutheran pastor in Fort Wayne, Indiana. The funeral services of the widowed Mrs. Meyer were held at Trinity Lutheran Church in Russellville, but she was interred in the cemetery of St. Paul's in Lohman. Her son passed away seven years later and was laid to rest in the cemetery of St. John's Lutheran Church in Fort Wayne, Indiana, where both he and his father had ministered.

Next to enter into the ministry at St. Paul's was Conrad Duerschner, who was installed sometime around Christmas 1867. He remained at the Lohman church for the next five years, and it was around the time of his departure that another major building activity began to unfold.

"In 1872 another church was built on the crest of the hill where our present church stands," writes Don Buchta. "The second church was built of stone quarried in the Lohman area. The members did virtually all of the construction." He added, "When it was completed, there were 63 families in the congregation. The cost was $4,716."

The original log church building was left standing and was utilized for several years as a schoolhouse for children of the congregation. Another important milestone in the church's history came in the late summer of 1875 with the arrival of Rev. George Fikenscher, who holds the distinction of being the longest-serving pastor for the church. Fikenscher's nearly thirty-year tenure leading his flock of faithful at St. Paul's included a new and unprecedented period of progress and growth for the church family. During his time at St. Paul's, Fikenscher also provided pastoral support to the small

From 1875 to 1904, Rev. George Fikenscher served as pastor for St. Paul's Lutheran Church and holds the distinction of being the longest-serving pastor in church history. *Gert Strobel.*

Lutheran church that was established in Centertown until such time as his responsibilities at his Lohman home church prevented him from continuing this rather demanding arrangement.

After his arrival, the first parsonage was erected. The first church building, the log structure that was being utilized as a schoolhouse, was disassembled in 1880, and a new brick schoolhouse was erected. According to the booklet printed in 1952 for the one hundredth anniversary of St. Paul's Lutheran Church, "From 1882 to 1904, Pastor Fikenscher conducted a full-fledged parochial school with teachings in secular as well as religious subjects." The school would later close, with students either receiving their coursework at nearby Lohman School or traveling to Jefferson City or Russellville, although the pastor would continue to provide two years of confirmation training and education.

In 1880, around the same time the new parochial school building was erected for the church, members of the congregation watched as a village grew up near the town that was now being supported by a railroad spur. The community soon earned the designation of Lohman in the early 1880s because of the post office established by businessman Charles W. Lohman, who was also of the Lutheran faith.

Then, in the year 1890, fifteen years following Pastor Fikenscher's arrival at St. Paul's, a second parsonage was built. Then, a few years later, the congregation of St. Paul's celebrated the establishment of a sister church, Trinity Evangelical Lutheran Church in Russellville. At the dedication for Trinity on September 13, 1896, Pastor Fikenscher spoke in the German language at the morning services, while the afternoon services were conducted in English.

Retiring from the ministry on December 31, 1904, Rev. Fikenscher spent his remaining years in the Lohman area. The German native was eighty-two years old when he died in 1922 and is interred in the cemetery of St. Paul's Lutheran Church. The year following Fikenscher's death, the decision was made to erect a new church due to the growth that had occurred in the congregation, much of which can be attributed to the late reverend's efforts.

"Time had taken its toll on the building by 1923 and more seating room was needed," the 110th anniversary booklet printed in 1962 explains. "After some debate about renovation, the governing fathers decided that a new church would be built. The congregation plunged into this undertaking wholeheartedly."

"Gus Linsenbardt, who served as foreman for the construction of the church, says that the stone steeple from the original church was retained

Pastor Fikensher (*back row, far left*) conducted a parochial school at St. Paul's from 1882 to 1904. *Gert Strobel.*

when the new church was built and that the steeple was covered with a brick veneer so that it would match the newly constructed brick church," reported the *Daily Capital News* on July 30, 1977. "Within nine months, the church was completed and was officially dedicated on November 16, 1924."

The cost of the new church, in addition to furnishings, totaled an estimated $23,000, which, through the dedication of the congregation, was a debt quickly erased. The next major construction project came in 1948, when work on a new parsonage was initiated. The old parsonage was demolished, and on June 26, 1949, the $18,000 new brick parsonage was dedicated. The next several years would bring improvements to the basement and the installation of updated heating and cooling systems for the church.

The Luther League became just one of many activities within the church that provided members of the congregation with means to actively support the work of their faith. Not only did these undertakings occur on the local level but they also included participation and support of the Lutheran League at the district, national and international levels. The organization of the Luther League at St. Paul's occurred in 1933 and grew to support many programs and projects that included Bible camps and raising funds for the Red Cross during World War II. The *Jefferson City Post-Tribune* reported on November 26, 1934, that the group put on the play *An Old-Fashioned Mother* at the hall in Lohman that later became known as the Lo-Mo Club. Members of the group would go on to perform assorted shows, comedies and three-act plays for the community in addition to hosting popular ice cream socials. Erwin Soell, a member of St. Paul's, attended the International Lutheran League convention in Pullman, Washington, in 1947, providing a report to his contemporaries on his return. During the celebration held in Lohman in 1976 to celebrate the nation's bicentennial, the Luther League from St. Paul's hosted an ice cream stand and entered a float in the parade. Many other groups were formed and remained active in the church, some under the umbrella of the Ladies Aid and the Junior Lutherans.

Gus Fischer Jr., a longtime member of the congregation at St. Paul's, was confirmed on April 9, 1952, and witnessed significant changes to the traditional services at the church. Records indicate that worship services were conducted entirely in German until the late 1920s.

"When I was real young, I can remember that there was a German service about once a month, but sometime around the late 1940s, that stopped entirely, and they were done in English only," Fischer said. "Also, I remember we used to take communion about once a quarter, but now that is done every Sunday."

In early 1998, Gus Fischer Jr. also chaired a building committee given the task of resolving a problem that was a blessing in disguise: developing plans for building a new addition to the church that would provide for more classrooms, storage, an office for the pastor, etc. Groundbreaking for the construction project occurred in July 1998, and by early summer the following year, there was a new addition on the east side of the church that provided 4,808 square feet of additional space. Like other major construction undertakings in the church's history, the $215,000 project was financed through pledges and generous donations from members of the congregation and supporters of St. Paul's. Also, savings—often uncalculated in such major construction initiatives—came from the many members of the congregation and community who graciously made donations of their various talents to ensure the project remained affordable and became a resounding success.

The church cemetery has also been an important part of St. Paul's history throughout the decades. The first recorded burial occurred in 1857 following the death of Anna Margaretta Plochberger. The cemetery continued to grow throughout the years, but it would not have been without the foresight and resources of an inconspicuous congregation member and his sister that it became a perpetual care cemetery. Otto John Strobel, who attended the church since his birth and was confirmed as a member in 1903, left a sizeable

Gertrude Raithel married Hugo Strobel in a ceremony at St. Paul's in 1967. She began serving as church organist in 1946 and, prior to her death in 2020, catalogued much of the congregation's history. *Eugene Strobel.*

endowment from his estate for the cemetery on his passing on December 20, 1962. Strobel's story is covered in greater detail in subsequent pages. The first records of the St. Paul's Perpetual Cemetery Fund, Inc., were established on August 20, 1963. Five charter members were selected, and their first step was to receive a certificate of incorporation as a not-for-profit corporation from the state. They then set a goal to grow the endowment fund to $3,000 prior to accepting maintenance of the cemetery, which was achieved in late 1963. The congregation of St. Paul's voted in 1967, during their annual meeting, to approve St. Paul's Perpetual Cemetery Fund, Inc., and thus accepted responsibility for the cemetery. Since that time, the cemetery fund has continued to grow through the donations, resulting in the necessary funds being available to make continued improvements.

The late Gertrude Strobel, who was ninety-six years old when she passed away in 2020, served in many capacities within the church but was best known for being the organist since 1946. An ardent devotee to her Lutheran faith, she embraced her abundant talent to compose the words of praise for the church's 100th anniversary celebration in 1952, awestruck by the longevity of the congregation that had been established by her German forebearers.

Loudly we sing, loudly we sing,
As the organ rolls forth loud and strong,
With ever joyful hearts we thank our God,
So join in the everlasting song.

Reflecting on the impact, both physical and spiritual, that St. Paul's has made throughout its decades of existence, historian Don Buchta explained, "Even though changes have been numerous over the years, one thing has remained constant: the faith of our founding fathers who laid the foundation for a church built on love, caring, faith and inspiration."

Embracing his hopes for the future of the congregation, Buchta concluded, "These values have been passed on to each generation and practiced faithfully throughout the years. Hopefully, they will continue to be a way of spiritual life for all who journey to the 'Church on the Hill' in Lohman, Missouri."

GUS FISCHER SR.

The late Oscar Handlin, noted American historian and professor of history at Harvard University, intuitively stated, "Once I thought to write a history of the immigrants in America. Then I discovered that the immigrants were American history."

These words describe groups of men and women clinging to the promise of opportunities in America, leaving the difficulties of their ancestral homelands with little to their name other than an entrenched work ethic and a dedication to providing for their families.

"My grandfather, John Fischer—he didn't have a middle name—was born in Germany on March 7, 1856," said Gus Fischer Jr. of Lohman. "He immigrated to the Millbrook area with his parents in 1865, when he was only nine years old."

Like many young German immigrants toiling the farmland in the vicinity, Gus's grandfather met a young woman, Margarethe Rockelman, and

A first-generation American citizen, John Gustav Fischer Sr. farmed in the Lohman area his entire life. He is pictured with his wife, the former Erma Linsenbardt, in 1917. *Gus Fischer Jr.*

married her in 1880. He embarked on his own life of farming while raising eight children, including John Gustav Fischer.

"My father, John 'Gus' Fischer Sr., was born in 1893 and grew up on a farm south of Millbrook," said Gus Fischer Jr. "He worked hard from an early age and had three brothers and four sisters. Back then, farmers didn't have the benefit of tractors and other farm equipment." Fischer Jr. continued, "There weren't many opportunities for education, and he talked about attending a one-room schoolhouse in Pleasant Hill. He only went there for about five years and said he could only go to class if he was able to cross the Moreau River....Sometimes the water was too high."

The family brought with them from Germany their Lutheran faith and, after settling near Millbrook, began attending St. Paul's Lutheran Church in Lohman. This religious tradition has carried forward with the Fischer family for more than four generations, with Gus Fischer Jr. and his wife members of the same congregation as his great-grandparents.

"Eventually, my grandfather gave all of his sons a farm," said Fischer Jr. "I was told that his daughters, instead of receiving farms, were given $5,000 each when they married."

Fischer Jr. recalled that the farm given to his father stretched across 133 acres between Stringtown and Lohman. In 1917, his father married the former Erma Linsenbardt, and the couple focused on building a home, raising a family and working to extract a living from their farm.

Jeanette, wife of Gus Fischer Jr., said, "My father-in-law built a cement house on the farm after he was married. We were told that they found some type of rock or slate here on the farm that they would burn for several days, and it could then be used for the cement The holes from where they dug the rock can still be seen here on the farm." Pausing, Jeanette added, "My father said that his dad helped him build the house; it was a two-story structure, and he talked about having to climb up a ladder with buckets full of cement to pour into the forms."

This became the home where Gus Fischer Jr. and his eight siblings—seven of whom made it into adulthood—were raised. His parents, though lacking disposable income, demonstrated a stalwart work ethic and ensured their children were never wanting for the necessities.

"Farming became a family effort; we planted those rocky hills outside Lohman with an alternating schedule of corn, wheat and oats," said Fischer Jr. "Sometimes, heavy rains would come and wash all of the seeds away that we had planted."

Growing up in a concrete house, Fischer explained, though it was certainly a stable structure, frequently offered its own set of challenges.

"We had a wood stove, and because there was no insulation, you had the one room that was warm in the winters, and all the others were freezing," he recalled. "There was a woodstove in the kitchen for cooking, too, so it wasn't too bad in there, either."

Fischer Sr. passed away in 1968; he and his wife are interred in the cemetery of St. Paul's Lutheran Church in Lohman. *Gus Fischer Jr.*

In addition to raising crops, his parents maintained around fifteen cows, six for milking and the rest for beef. Additionally, his father was for several years the treasurer for the German Mutual Insurance Company, which continues to serve the insurance needs of policyholders throughout Mid-Missouri. In 1931, Gus Fischer Sr. was reelected to the board of the Stringtown District School. The following year, he built a service station/tavern on his farm near the junction of Highways C and D south of Lohman. He rented the building for several years and later added an outdoor wooden dance floor. Musical entertainment was provided by local musicians Vic and Oscar Linsenbardt.

"My parents often spoke German around the house and with others in the community because that was really their first language," said Fischer Jr. "[My father] also had the saying, 'You have to know what you can do.'"

Gus Fischer Sr. welcomed progress when electricity came to the Lohman area in 1947. In later years, he purchased a small tractor to replace his earlier reliance on mules and horses. The first-generation U.S. citizen died in 1968 and was laid to rest in the cemetery of St. Paul's Lutheran Church; his wife joined him in rest thirteen years later. Living on a section of the farm once owned by his parents, Fischer Jr. recognizes that the tireless labors of early immigrants to the area have helped provide the more comfortable lifestyle currently enjoyed by their descendants.

"My great-grandparents, grandparents and parents toiled all of their lives and all experienced hard times," said Fischer Jr. "My mother lost two of her daughters—my sisters—at a young age, and that had to be very trying for her." He added, "Theirs might not be a unique story coming from early Lohman and Stringtown history, but they all struggled to survive one day at a time and built a better life for others."

Christian Soell

Many names are written in early chapters of Lohman history, highlighting the people who established the foundation of this rural Cole County community. The late Christian Soell, a respected businessman, became more than a footnote in this fascinating historical account and made significant contributions during a period of the town's economic prosperity.

Born in Germany on January 30, 1881, Soell was reputed to have received an excellent education in his homeland. In 1896, when only fifteen years old, he immigrated to the United States and settled in Lohman, where his sister was residing.

"I have always heard that my grandfather, Christian Soell, had his passage to America paid by his older sister, Sophie," said Carol Beck. "He apparently arrived penniless because he purchased a box of sandwiches to last him on the train ride and also bought a 25-cent harmonica. After he missed his stop in Jefferson City, a man by the name of Brandt, who was employed by the railroad, helped get him to his sister's house."

After young Christian had attended school in Stringtown for only a few days, his sister advised him to quit wasting his time in classes since he already possessed as much knowledge and education as the teacher. In an effort to scratch out a living in his new homeland, Soell began working on the Stringtown-area farm of his older brother-in-law, Fred Lochner. He soon met and developed romantic interests in a young woman living on a neighboring farm, Anna Margaretha "Margaret" Kautsch.

Christian Soell immigrated to Lohman from Germany in 1896 and is best known for establishing Soell & Plochberger, a general mercantile store that contributed to the community's self-sufficiency. *Carol Beck.*

"Adam Kautsch, a well-established farmer, wasn't happy about having his daughter courted by a young man who was yet to prove his worth," wrote Erwin, the youngest of Soell's children. "I'm not sure when the courting started, but it was apparently by letter. During some of those years, he would write letters and leave them under a tub in the Kautsch smokehouse where Margaret would find and answer him."

Soell's first wife, the former Anna Margaretha Kautsch, was only forty-two when she died from ovarian cancer in 1927. *Carol Beck.*

Through patience, dedication and demonstrated work ethic, Soell was given Margaret's hand in marriage in a ceremony held at St. John's Lutheran Church in Stringtown on April 4, 1905. Prior to his marriage, Soell also worked for a couple of years at a general store in Lohman. On December 4, 1904, when only twenty-three years old, the aspiring businessman took a great risk by going into debt to purchase the general store from Peter Kiessling.

"The general merchandise stores in Lohman have traditionally been the heart of the business life of the community, making the town relatively self-sufficient with a wide range of goods," notes a Lohman historical booklet printed in 1976.

In 1910, Otto Kirchner bought into the store, which became a business partnership lasting only two years. Then, in 1913, Otto J.F. Plochberger (who married the sister of Soell's wife) purchased Kirchner's shares and became a co-owner. For more than three decades, Soell & Plochberger served as an important cog in Lohman's economic base and embraced the slogan "Every day is a bargain day."

As the years passed, Soell and his wife were active members of St. Paul's Lutheran Church in Lohman while also becoming parents to one son and five daughters: Oswald, Alma, Martha, Bertha, Wiltrud and Esther.

Erwin Soell explained that in addition to his father's work as a storekeeper, he "was a notary public and did a lot of legal work now done by attorneys. He drew up deeds, wills, promissory notes, etc., in addition to putting his notary seal on other legal documents."

In 1911, a year following the official incorporation of Lohman, Soell demonstrated his commitment to community betterment when elected to the position of town clerk. He went on to serve in this capacity longer than anyone else in the town's history. A dark moment came on January 2, 1927, when Soell's forty-two-year-old wife passed away after being hospitalized for several months with ovarian cancer. She was interred in the cemetery of St. Paul's Lutheran Church. Still reeling from the loss of their mother, Soell's children helped keep the store running and ensured household tasks were completed. Soon, the widower was informed by relatives living in Germany of a woman with no children whose fiancé had been killed in World War I.

After the death of his first wife in 1927, Soell married Margaret Marie Muller, a German woman whose fiancé had been killed in World War I. *Carol Beck.*

Margaret Marie Muller "received her first letter from [Soell] in November 1927," wrote Erwin. "By March 1928, she had agreed to come to New York and meet Dad." The couple married at St. Paul's Lutheran Church on November 24, 1928, once again providing Soell's children with a mother and he a wife. On August 11, 1931, Erwin Soell was born, becoming the only child born to this union.

Christian Soell left the mercantile business in 1945, selling his shares to his partner, Otto Plochberger, and his son, Martin Plochberger. The store was later sold to J.R. Strobel, who continued operating it as a general merchandise store for three decades. In his retirement, Soell continued his notary work, completed income tax forms and sold Hartford Insurance. He was sixty-nine years old when he died after suffering a heart attack driving to a doctor's appointment in Jefferson City. He was laid to rest in the cemetery at St. Paul's Lutheran Church alongside his first wife. When his second wife passed in 1982, she was buried in the same burial plot as Soell.

Reflecting on a grandfather of whom she has few memories, Carol Beck maintained she has relied on stories from friends and family to help her know the man who was Christian Soell.

Smiling, she said, "I remember getting to sit on his lap when he had a wicker rocking chair. He died when I was only in the first grade, and I don't remember a lot about him, but hearing stories and reading about him has helped me feel as though I have been given a chance to get to know him."

OTTO JOHN STROBEL

It could be said of the late Otto John Strobel that he was truly a person who gave of himself in both life and death. Not only did he serve his country in a distinguished manner in World War I, but after his passing years later, he also donated his entire estate to ensure a perpetual care cemetery could be established at St. Paul's Lutheran Church in his hometown of Lohman. Yet despite all of this benevolence, Strobel is perhaps best remembered for the trips he made to Jefferson City so that he could participate in meetings with the local Veterans of Foreign War Post—a twenty-eight-mile round trip he made by walking.

"The history of Strobel's walking feat actually got its start on the battlefields of France in 1918," reported the *Sunday News and Tribune* in its April 25, 1937 edition. "Marching was nothing unusual for the soldiers in those stirring days, and Strobel performed his duties so well he returned to America after the war with five medals for valor."

Prior to the veteran gaining attention because of his lengthy strolls to Jefferson City, his life story began on a small farm in the Lohman area where he was born on May 9, 1889.

"He spent his entire life in Lohman—except for the time he was in the army," said Lohman historian Gert Strobel. "He was also very dedicated to his faith and really enjoyed being a member of St. Paul's [Lutheran Church]."

Months after America's declaration of war against Germany in 1917, the twenty-eight-year-old Strobel was selected to serve his country. He was inducted into the U.S. Army in Jefferson City on September 20, 1917, and for the first time in his life left the county he had called home, bound for destinations unknown. According to his military service card, accessed through the Missouri State Archives, the recruit spent less than two months at Camp Funston, Kansas, where he trained with Company M, 356th Infantry—a company that drafted several men from the Cole County area.

Though he was among acquaintances from the Lohman area during his initial training, Strobel's tenure with the company was brief since he was transferred as a replacement to Battery B, 335th Field Artillery, at Camp Pike, Arkansas, on November 6, 1917. In March 1918, he again bid farewell to whatever friends had been able to make while at Camp Pike when he was transferred to Battery D, 102nd Field Artillery Regiment, and traveled to Camp Merritt, New Jersey. Shortly after his arrival, he boarded a troopship that set sail for an overseas warzone.

Now part of the 26th Division, Strobel and the soldiers of the 102nd were members of "the first complete American Division to be committed in France in 1918," notes *The Unit History of the 26th Division,* accessible through the website of the 26th Infantry "Yankee" Division. The website also notes that the division took part in six major campaigns of the war and "was cited [for their performance in combat] thirteen times by France, and three times by American Army Headquarters" in addition to spending 210 days fighting—the longest of all the American infantry divisions.

Returning from the war in April 1919, Gert Strobel notes, the combat-hardened soldier lived on his family's farm along with his only sibling, a sister named Antonia. In the years after the war, Strobel gained a reputation for being a hard worker, although the community's perceptions of him often limited the type of employment he was provided.

"He was not very good at communicating with people," said Gert Strobel, "which led many people to believe that because of the way he expressed himself, he might have some type of mental impairment. All he was ever really given was menial work around town, but he was really a very bright man—an avid reader who was truly self-educated."

The late John "Otto" Strobel was raised in the Lohman community and served in World War I. After the war, he gained a level of local notoriety for walking from Lohman to Jefferson City to attend VFW meetings. *Gert Strobel.*

Newspaper accounts note that the former artillery soldier became an active member of the VFW Post 1003 in Jefferson City in the mid-1930s and even served as the post surgeon, although the duties associated with this position were not clearly described. The veteran's most interesting postwar endeavors were his journeys to the VFW post's bimonthly meetings, utilizing as his path the railroad tracks of the former Bagnell Branch of the Missouri Pacific Railroad that once lay between Lohman and Jefferson City.

"Every two weeks for the last twenty-eight months he has awakened around 3 a.m., garbed himself in his uniform cap and trod the fourteen miles from his home to the city," as was explained in the April 25, 1937 edition of the *Sunday News and Tribune.*

The article further noted that Strobel—a self-described "astute student of political science"—would arrive in the city several hours prior to the meeting so that he could spend time at the library reading books in both English and German.

"He loved to talk about his military service, and when he got to the VFW, he felt right at home," said Gert Strobel. "After some of the meetings, the people at the capitol knew he was coming and would let him spend the night on one of the benches inside. The next morning, he would get up and walk all the way back to Lohman along the railroad tracks."

Strobel passed away at the Veterans' Hospital in St. Louis on December 20, 1962, at seventy-three years of age and was laid to rest in the cemetery of St. Paul's Lutheran Church, where he had been a lifelong member. Even in his passing, this often-misunderstood veteran was able to help provide for his community.

"He and his sister never made a lot of money in their lives, but they never spent anything either—if they had ten cents, they would save nine cents of it," said Gert Strobel. "When both he and his sister died, they gave their entire estate, a pretty good sum of money, to the church so that a perpetual care cemetery could be established." She continued, "Nobody ever paid much attention to him, but he gave a lot to both his country and this community. Since neither he nor his sister ever married or had any children, there has really been no one to carry on his memory, and that is a shame considering what he did for the community and his service in the war."

CHAPTER 4

CENTRAL CHURCH (JEFFERSON CITY)

An Early House of Worship for German Immigrants

A s one of the oldest Protestant congregations established in Cole County, the German Evangelical Central Church—now known as Central Church—for many years served as a house of Christian worship for German immigrants who had been associated with two separate denominations prior to their relocation to the United States. It is part of a historical legacy linked to King Frederic William III of Prussia, who, in 1817, on the three hundredth anniversary of the Reformation, unified the Reformed (Calvinist) and Lutheran churches. This unification later inspired the emigration of Germans seeking religious freedoms, many of whom eventually settled in Central Missouri.

"The German Evangelical Central congregation is a member of the German Evangelical Synod of North America, a church association which advocates the union of two branches of the Protestant church, the Lutheran and Reformed," explains the *Illustrated Sketchbook and Directory of Jefferson City and Cole County*.

Although it was several years before official organization took place, the congregation of the German Evangelical Central Church, part of the Reformed movement, began to materialize in Jefferson City in 1850, the same year that a piece of property was purchased on a hill on the corner of Ashley and Washington Streets. The aforementioned book adds, "The congregation at Jefferson City was organized…[in] 1858, but for more than two years was without a regular pastor, services being conducted at certain intervals by itinerant preachers. The meetings were held in private houses until 1859, when a plain brick church was built at a cost of about $1,500."

German Evangelical Church Jefferson City, Mo.

The second church building of German Evangelical Central Church in Jefferson City, now Central Church, is pictured on this vintage postcard. In 1903, the church helped plant the seed of what became Friedens Church Brazito. *Jeremy P. Ämick.*

The first full-time pastor for the fledgling church was Rev. Joseph Rieger, who accepted the call in the spring of 1860. Funds were then raised to build a parsonage for the new pastor and his family, which was completed in late summer of the same year. Under the pastorate of Rieger, the congregation began to grow. In 1868, Rev. Edward Huber, a Swiss native and graduate of Eden Seminary in Marthasville, was appointed as an assistant to Rev. Rieger.

"Rev. Rieger died at the parsonage, August 20, 1869, with his wife, daughter, and Rev. Huber attending him," explains the Central United Church of Christ sesquicentennial history from 2008.

Rev. Rieger, who had ushered the congregation through the tumultuous years of the Civil War and had helped found Eden Theological Seminary for Evangelical pastors, was interred in Central Evangelical Cemetery. His remains were moved to Riverview Cemetery in the mid-1960s after the expansion of US Highway 54 consumed the cemetery property.

In 1869, Rev. Huber was unanimously elected to succeed the late Rev. Rieger. As the years passed, many of those who identified as Lutherans and who had been attending worship services at Central left the congregation when Trinity Lutheran Church organized in Jefferson City in 1870. It was also during Huber's tenure at Central that the church's parochial school was erected in 1872. Rev. Huber continued to serve the Central congregation until 1874 but went on to receive widespread acclaim for seeking a reunification of German Protestants.

"Rev. Edward Huber, formerly chaplain of the Missouri Legislature, hopes to see the day when the two branches of the Lutheran Church will be united, and is doing all within his power to bring about that end," reported the *St. Louis Post-Dispatch* on August 20, 1899.

Following the departure of Rev. Huber in 1874, several pastors came to serve the Reformed congregation for short periods. Pastor J.U. Schneider was welcomed to the church in 1888 and soon sought to plant the seed of a new congregation in an outlying community.

Historical documents from Friedens Church Brazito explain, "On September 1, 1889, the Reverend J.U. Schneider, who was then the pastor of Central Church, 'was given permission to cancel one evening service of worship each month in order to enable him to try to organize a Christian congregation in Brazito.'" This endeavor did come to fruition under Pastor Schneider's tenure at Central Church.

A major milestone in church history arrived in 1891 when the congregation, which had experienced substantial growth, embarked on the undertaking of erecting a new church.

"The contract for the new church was awarded to Mr. Fred Binder, the president of the congregation," notes the *Illustrated Sketchbook and Directory of Jefferson City and Cole County*. "With pardonable pride the congregation may point to its substantial and beautiful church edifice, which has been erected and furnished at a cost of $10,000."

A second parsonage was built in 1898 on the site of the previous one. Five years later, under the leadership of Rev. Charles Hoffman of Central Church, a new church was finally built and dedicated in the community of Brazito. The next century delivered many changes, such as the closure of the parochial school and the construction of a large Sunday school building with classrooms. The name of the congregation changed to Central Evangelical and Reformed Church following a merger of two synods in 1934.

The contractor for the second church building of Central Church was Frederick Binder, who was involved in the construction of many historical buildings in surrounding areas. *Central Church.*

A second merger in 1961 resulted in it being renamed Central United Church of Christ. Buildings have since been demolished and new additions erected in the interceding years, but the original sanctuary built in 1891 remains a principal element of the church campus. More recently, the congregation underwent another name change and is now Central Church. The legacy of the congregation, however, remains steeped in a fascinating story of German immigrants seeking to establish their religious identity in a foreign land.

As Rev. Dr. Stephen H. Bucholz notes in the forward he wrote for the church's 150th anniversary in 2008, "Jefferson City was a small, bustling town, the seat of state government, and a magnet for German immigrants and settlers....These folks decided to establish a church of their heritage and theological persuasion that they had known in their homeland." Nodding to the past with hopes for a bountiful future, he adds, "May our current generation and our posterity continue to keep the faith so the question of the wisdom of the Proverbs will be answered affirmatively, 'Will our faith have children?'"

CHAPTER 5

ST. JOHN'S LUTHERAN CHURCH

(STRINGTOWN)

Rising from the Ashes of Controversy in 1867

During the Civil War, dissension began to foment within the congregation of St. Paul's Lutheran Church in Lohman, organized in 1852 by German immigrants. Doctrinal disputes resulted in the decision of some congregants to leave the Missouri Synod and join the Iowa Synod. Choosing to maintain an association with the Missouri Synod, several of the founding members of St. Paul's split away from the church and later organized St. John's Lutheran Church in nearby Stringtown on July 24, 1867.

Pastor Gerald Scheperle, who was baptized at St. John's Lutheran Church in Stringtown and later confirmed and ordained at Trinity Lutheran Church in Jefferson City, explained, "From what I was told, the organization of St. John's in Stringtown took place in the house now owned by my brother, Mark Scheperle. The stone house was built in 1854 and belonged to one of the Kautsch family members who was among the group that split away from St. Paul's. The house is still standing [on Stringtown Station Road]."

"For the founders of St. John's…this was the second organizing procedure in which they had taken part in a fifteen-year period," explains a booklet printed in celebration of the St. John's sesquicentennial celebration in 2017. The booklet adds, "Since the members who withdrew their memberships from their former congregation were on their own and desiring to remain in the Lutheran Church-Missouri Synod, they accepted the services of Pastor [Emil] Wege, who was pastor of Zion Lutheran Church, Jefferson City." Pastor Wege was also serving groups of Lutherans at Honey Creek

In 1867, following a split from St. Paul's Lutheran in Church in Lohman over doctrinal disputes, a small group organized St. John's Lutheran Church in Stringtown. *Jeremy P. Ämick.*

and in Jefferson City, although the churches in those areas had yet to be officially organized.

A church constitution, written in German, was approved, while a frame church was constructed to provide a worship site for the fledgling congregation. As the church continued to grow, several pastors answered the call to serve at St. John's while also serving Zion Lutheran Church and, in the ensuing years, conducted baptisms, confirmations and burials, these last in a new cemetery established near the church. Additionally, like many Lutheran pastors of the era, they conducted worship services in the German language.

The first church building lasted only eight years before being struck by lightning in 1872 and burning to the ground. The second church, another wood frame structure, was erected the same year and would provide a home to the congregation for the next thirty-three years. Finally, in the late 1870s, the congregation had grown to the extent that St. John's finally had the

The first church building for St. John's lasted only eight years after being struck by lightning. Pictured is the second church, a frame structure built in 1872. *St. John's Lutheran, Stringtown.*

resources to call their first resident pastor, a German native by the name of William Steinrauf.

Previous to his arrival at St. John's in Stringtown, Pastor Steinrauf was described in the *German Valley Bulletin* on August 3, 1956, as "a traveling missionary who resided in Pecatonica [Illinois] and introduced himself to his fellow Lutherans. Pastor Steinrauf happened to be in Pecatonica because the freight train on which he was traveling 'would go no further.'" The congregation of St. John's Lutheran Church, organized in 1875, asked Pastor Steinrauf to be their resident pastor, a call he accepted until coming to St. John's in Stringtown a couple of years later.

Pastor Steinrauf remained with the Stringtown congregation for approximately a year. The *Republican-Northwestern* noted on October 15, 1918, that he later served Immanuel Lutheran Church in Belvidere, Illinois, before making the career change to become a physician. Dr. Steinrauf was sixty-eight years old when he passed away on October 12, 1918, and is interred in Saint Peter's Cemetery in St. Louis County, Missouri. Although he remained for only a year with St. John's Lutheran Church in Stringtown, his brief tenure there represents a turning point in the church's history, since it demonstrated the congregation had the resources to support a resident pastor and no longer needed to rely on Zion Lutheran Church.

Following Pastor Steinrauf's departure, Pastor Vetter of Immanuel Lutheran Church in Honey Creek served as interim pastor at St. John's while the congregation focused on the process of locating a new resident pastor to fill their pulpit vacancy, who arrived in 1880: Pastor John A. Proft, from Texas.

Regrettably, tragedy occurred fifteen years after the church's founding while Pastor John August Proft was serving as pastor for the congregation. His wife, Dorothea Margaretha Henrietta, died during childbirth on April 17, 1882, when only thirty years old. She was laid to rest in the church cemetery under a beautiful monument featuring an angel pointing to the heavens while comforting a small girl. Pastor Proft's fascinating legacy is discussed in detail in the following pages.

"In 1902, it was concluded that the frame church had become inadequate, for it needed many major and costly repairs and was difficult to heat," notes a church pamphlet printed in 1955. "So, the decision was made to begin planning for its replacement."

A building fund was established, and it was resolved by the congregation to replace the frame structure with a new church made from brick and stone. John J. Scheperle Sr., a member of the congregation who had helped erect Centennial Mill in nearby Millbrook, was chosen to serve as the architect and builder of the new church, and the cornerstone was laid on May 14, 1905. Church records indicate that Scheperle modeled the new church of St. John's by incorporating features used by other area Lutheran churches. The floor plan of the church was similar to that used by St. Paul's Lutheran Church in California, while the north entrance was almost identical to that of the second Trinity Lutheran Church in Jefferson City. Also, the balcony that still exists on the three sides of the interior of St. John's Lutheran Church was fashioned after that of Immanuel Lutheran Church in Honey Creek, which had been designed years earlier by St. John's pastor Johann Proft.

"All the lumber used in the building of the church was donated in the form of logs, which were milled and prepared, free of charge, by the architect and builder, Mr. John Scheperle Sr.," the church's one-hundredth-anniversary booklet states.

Stone for the foundation was quarried east of the cemetery on property still owned by the church, and a large part of the lumber was donated, while the bricks were purchased. Construction began in the spring of 1905. Later that year, on December 10, 1905, dedication services were held, with Scheperle presenting the key to the church door to Pastor John

The third church building of St. John's Lutheran Church is pictured under construction in 1905, at which point it was ready for installation of the steeple. Standing next to the ladder (*at left*) is John Scheperle Sr., architect and builder. *Susan Scheperle Schenewerk.*

H. Mueller. The cost of the project after all the construction was completed came to $2,644.70. Members of the congregation had graciously donated $2,649.70 toward the project—a sum that, much like building endeavors of other Lutheran churches, fails to account for the donation of time and materials by volunteers. Since it was determined that the cost of an altar, pulpit and lectern would be around $200, Pastor John Mueller graciously employed his skills as a woodworker to build the altar and pulpit, while another member of the congregation assembled the lectern. This altar was used until 1918, at which time a new one was donated by the wife of Mr. John Heinrich. It is uncertain what became of the altar constructed by Pastor Mueller.

Gerald Scheperle, long-serving pastor of St. John's Lutheran Church in Schubert, shared the following story regarding the construction of the 1905 church building that is still being used to this day by the congregation at St. John's in Stringtown.

"When my grandfather, Herman Kautsch, was a young kid, they used his father's [Adam Kautsch] barn about a mile or so from the church to assemble the large side windows for the church," Scheperle said. "From what I was told, my great-grandfather, Joseph Scheperle, was a carpenter and helped his brother John Scheperle Sr. in construction of the church.

This Christmas photograph from prior to 1918 shows the altar built by Pastor John Mueller. Church history notes that since real candles were used on the Christmas tree, a congregation member sat in front with a bucket of water and a rag in case it caught fire. *Susan Scheperle Schenewerk.*

They were both Swabian and spoke Swabian German, with is a very unique dialect. The Kautsch family came from Bavaria and spoke a different dialect of German. Apparently, John and Joseph would get into arguments while working together on the church, but since they were arguing in Swabian, none of the Kautsch family that were helping could understand what was being said."

The congregation of St. John's Lutheran Church has successfully maintained this aged church building, but there have been additions and remodeling to the original structure throughout the last several decades. In the years prior to World War II, there was a German phrase inscribed around the upper part of the chancel that featured the words of Luke 11:28. It stated, "Ja, selig sind, die das Wort Gottes hören und bewahren": "Yes, blessed are those who hear and keep the world of God."

Major updates to the church building itself came eighty years after its initial construction. In 1985, additions were built to the church, including an office for the pastor, enlargement of the narthex, a youth room above the narthex, a room for parents, a storage room and restrooms.

"When I was younger, I can remember that we had about one church service in German every month," said Edgar Kautsch, a member of the 1949 confirmation class for St. John's. His father, Gustav Kautsch, was confirmed at the church in 1914.

Reflecting on the many changes he's witnessed in the last several decades, Kautsch added, "The men used to sit on the right side of the church and the women on the left. There also used to be communion about once a month, then it went to every other Sunday and now it's done every Sunday."

A parsonage was erected in 1898 to provide a home for the pastors and their families. This was replaced in 1913 with a second parsonage, built by John Scheperle Jr., the son of the builder of the current church. This parsonage has undergone several updates but is still utilized for its original purpose of providing a home to the resident pastor and his family.

Fifty-one-year-old Ernest Heinrich Runge, a native of Concordia, Missouri, accepted a call to St. John's Lutheran Church and was installed on April 10, 1927, thus beginning his stint as the second-longest-serving pastor in church history. He had previously been the pastor of Zion Lutheran Church in Blackburn, Missouri, where he also taught for the congregation's Christian Day School and provided pastoral leadership for a Lutheran mission in nearby Marshall. Possessing a good grasp of the German language, he often preached sermons in both German and English. It was in 1943, Pastor Runge's next-to-last year in the pulpit, that the decision was made to

Pastor Fred H. Reininga (*back row, center*) is pictured with students of the parochial school at St. John's Lutheran Church in April 1926. *Ethel Heidbreder.*

have only one monthly service in German due to the unpopularity of the language because of its association with the war raging in Europe. Within two years, the decision was made by the congregation to begin holding all worship services entirely in English.

"Pastor Runge's faithfulness is attested by the fact that only once during his twenty-seven years as a teacher did he [ever] dismiss a class, and that dismissal was brought about from severe burns he suffered when the parsonage caught fire in 1927," St. John's 150th anniversary book notes. "Mrs. Runge was attending her oldest daughter at the time, which was shortly after the death of her first child."

Retiring from St. John's in the spring of 1944 at the age of sixty-eight, Runge went on to serve as assistant pastor of Immanuel Lutheran Church in Palatine, Illinois, until suffering a severe stroke in late 1951. Due to his medical condition, he relocated to Blackburn and died on February 14, 1955. He was laid to rest in the cemetery of Zion Lutheran Church in Blackburn, the congregation he had served for twenty years prior to coming to Stringtown. His legacy of Christian dedication continued through his son, Ernest Louis Runge, who followed the path of his father by also attending seminary and becoming a Lutheran pastor.

Ortwin Runge was three years old when his father, Pastor Ernest Runge, was installed at St. John's in 1927. When his father retired from St. John's,

Ortwin was preparing to turn twenty-one and had spent the majority of his formative years as a member of the congregation. In the 1970s, Ortwin commissioned a painting of St. John's Lutheran Church as it appeared during the period of his father's ministry and gave it as an anniversary gift to his wife. His sister-in-law, Victoria Runge, an accomplished artist, created the painting, which features the original 1905 church prior to the 1985 additions while also showing the schoolhouse and parsonage. For many years, it hung in the home of Ortwin Runge, who passed away in 2000. His wife, Norma, requested that the painting be given to St. John's Lutheran Church following her death, which occurred in 2016.

Like many before him, Pastor Runge not only served as St. John's pastor but was also the primary teacher at the parochial school. Providing a parochial education to the students of the congregation was a focus of Christian life that became evident early in St. John's history. The first schoolhouse was a whitewashed wooden building erected in 1894. In 1915, it was replaced by a brick schoolhouse that taught "the four Rs": reading, writing, arithmetic and religion.

"I attended my first three years of classes at Stringtown School before starting classes at the St. John's schoolhouse," Edgar Kautsch recalled. "I

This painting features St. John's Lutheran Church as it appeared during the pastorate of Ernest Runge, who was installed in 1927. The painting was donated to the church in 2016 and is displayed in the parish hall. *Jeremy P. Ämick.*

attended the church school for four years until Pastor [Clifford] Bliss left in the late 1940s. Then I completed the eighth grade at Lohman and then went to Russellville High School."

The school at St. John's closed in 1952 following consolidation of local school districts. The school building, since it was no longer being used, began to deteriorate over the years and was torn down by a contractor in 1990. A small canopy has since been dedicated at the site of the former schoolhouse, which features a picture of the brick school and displays the bell once used to signal students to classes.

An important moment in local Lutheran history came in the late 1970s when the congregation at Zion Lutheran Church chose to disband because of declining membership. The altar, pulpit and lectern from Zion were then donated to St. John's. The painting of Jesus with his right hand raised in blessing was removed from the altar received from Zion and replaced with a painting of Jesus rescuing Peter from the raging sea, which had been removed from St. John's old altar. The painting of Jesus that was removed from the Zion altar was cut, framed and now hangs near the door that once served as the primary entrance to St. John's Lutheran Church.

Built in 1915, this was the second of two schoolhouses used to provide an education to students in the congregation. This building was torn down in 1990. *St. John's Lutheran, Stringtown.*

St. John's Lutheran Church continues to use the altar received after Zion Lutheran Church closed in the late 1970s. *Jeremy P. Ämick.*

Along with the additions made to the "1905 church," the former parish hall that had been built in 1938 was demolished and a new one constructed in 1995. In 1985, Pastor Warren Brandt, a Wisconsin native and U.S. Air Force veteran, answered the call to serve at St. John's. He remained with the congregation for twenty-eight years and is thus far the longest-serving pastor in the history of St. John's Lutheran Church.

Generations of local residents continue to pass through the doors of St. John's Lutheran Church for worship and fellowship. It is a heritage, as noted in the 100th anniversary booklet printed in 1967, highlighted by an impressive legacy of service to family and the Lord and a dedication to the care of a church building that has become a historical landmark in the community. St. John's Lutheran Church now maintains the distinction of being the longest-operating church of the Missouri Synod in Cole County and the surrounding areas.

The church's one-hundredth-anniversary booklet notes, "O, what beauty, therefore, is found in each and every footstep which we would trace as we open our 'History Book of God's Love,' and, by His Spirit, see how He would write each 'Year of His Grace' indelibly upon our souls…"

JOHN JACOB KAUTSCH

A few miles south of Lohman along Stringtown Station Road is a farm belonging to Berdene and Lonnie Thompson and possessing a legacy dating to 1851. It was at this time that Johan (John) Jacob Kautsch, who had only recently emigrated from Germany, settled in the Lohman area. He would go on to not only establish a farm that remains in the Kautsch family but also help organize two Lutheran Churches that remain vibrant parts of their communities.

"We know from the original land grant certificates that John J. Kautsch homesteaded this property in 1851 and it was purchased in two tracts," said Berdene Thompson, discussing her great-grandfather. "There was a log cabin built on the property from hand-hewn logs that were secured with wooden pegs. The current house we live in was built around the cabin, and it has been expanded upon in later years."

Farming proved to be a difficult endeavor for a single man toiling in the years prior to tractors and similar implements. Regardless, Kautsch maintained a focus on faith and family, which was evidenced by his dedication to ensuring a house of worship existed for the German Lutherans making the area their new home.

Left: Gust Kautsch is pictured on his wedding day in 1932 with his wife, Agnes Jungmeyer. His grandfather, Johan Jacob Kautsch, helped organize the Lutheran churches in Lohman and Stringtown. *Berdene Thompson.*

Right: John Sebastian Kautsch married Susanna "Amelia" Loesch in 1894. His father, Johan Jacob, immigrated to the Lohman area in the late 1840s. *Berdene Thompson.*

In the fall of 1852, through the guidance of Pastor J.P. Kalb from Zion Lutheran Church, south of Jefferson City, John Kautsch met in the home of John A. Plochberger with four other men to discuss the formation of a new church.

"They established their congregation on the basis of the Word of God, both Old and New Testaments, as the sole rule and norm of faith and life," explained a booklet printed in 1952 to celebrate the one hundredth anniversary of the founding of St. Paul's Lutheran Church in Lohman.

John's older brother, Andreas Kautsch, who had immigrated to the Lohman area in the late 1840s, also took an active role in the development of the new church. On August 17, 1853, conveyance records reveal, John Kautsch transferred forty acres of property to the trustees of the new church—John A. Plochberger and Andreas Kautsch—for the construction of "St. Paul Church."

Several of John J. Kautsch's siblings eventually immigrated to the Lohman area, including his younger brother, Ehrhardt. On October 8, 1864, Ehrhardt was killed during an encounter with General Sterling Price's forces outside of Lohman and was buried in the cemetery of St. Paul's Lutheran Church.

It was around the time of his brother's death that "dissension arose in the congregation at Lohman over certain points of doctrine which members of St. Paul's could not and would not subscribe to," explains the booklet printed in 1867 for the 100th anniversary of St. John's Lutheran Church in Stringtown. The booklet further notes that "a number of the members of St. Paul's could not agree to the terms of settlement which were proposed and voted to leave St. Paul's and organize a congregation which would remain loyal to the Lutheran Church—Missouri Synod."

John Jacob Kautsch and his growing family were among those who left to establish St. John's Lutheran Church in Stringtown.

In 1866, Kautsch and his wife welcomed a new son into the world, John Sebastian. He was introduced to hard work on the farm while also being raised in the new St. John's Lutheran Church, being confirmed as a member in 1880.

"My grandfather John Sebastian Kautsch purchased the farm from his father for $1,000," said Berdene Thompson.

The Kautsch family patriarch, John Jacob, was laid to rest in the cemetery in St. John's Lutheran Church following his death in 1909. At the time, his grandson, Gust, was only nine years old but already learning to toil on the farm established by his grandfather while also being actively raised in the Lutheran faith.

"When my father, Gust Kautsch, was confirmed at St. John's Lutheran Church in 1914, he was one of the confirmation classes to receive all of their instruction entirely in the German language," said Berdene Kautsch. "Sometime around 1920, they started doing the instruction in English," she added.

An interesting feature of the farm, explained Berdene, which was likely built during the ownership of John Sebastian Kautsch, is a corncrib that has since had a metal shed constructed around it. The corncrib, much like the old log cabin on the farm, was constructed with hand-hewn logs held together with large wooden pegs.

Gust married Agnes Jungmeyer in 1932 and worked the family farm during the difficult years of the Great Depression. In 1936, they welcomed their first child, Edgar, followed by two daughters—Berdene and Margie—several years later.

Following the death of John Sebastian Kautsch in 1940, Gust continued to work the farm while also helping care for his mother, Amelia. When his mother passed in 1962, he purchased his sister's part of the property after inheriting the remainder. Throughout the years, the size of the farm has changed because of purchases and sales. However, Berdene Thompson lives on a section of the original farm property purchased by her grandfather, while her siblings live on sections purchased by their father in later years.

The story of the Kautsch farm, Berdene explained, may parallel that of many early immigrants who came to mid-Missouri in search of a better life, but it also has an interesting connection to the formation of two churches.

"Our great-grandfather made a living farming like many in the area did at that time, but it is fascinating that he helped establish St. Paul's Lutheran Church and then St. John's Lutheran Church," she said. "It must have been a busy time in his life and throughout the communities of Stringtown and Lohman, and his influence lives on because both of these churches are still going strong to this day."

Pastor Johann Proft

The Wendish are an interesting people who, despite never possessing an independent nation and being surrounded by Germans, were able to maintain a unique identity. In the mid-1800s, many Wendish emigrated from their homeland in East Germany and settled, for the most part, in areas of Australia and Texas. Yet one Wendish pastor eventually arrived in Missouri, experiencing great personal strife but leaving his mark through churches he designed.

Johann "John" August Proft was born in Maltitz, Saxony (Germany), on June 19, 1844. According to a historical sketch written by his great-grandson, Robert Proft, he "was ten years old when the Wends from his neighborhood boarded the Ben Nevis for Texas."

These neighbors would provide an anchor for Proft's own future migration to the United States. However, for the next several years, he remained in Saxony, receiving a traditional elementary education and learning rudimentary elements of design by completing an apprenticeship as a cabinetmaker. However, he later enrolled in Hermannsburg Mission Society School in Hanover after revealing an affinity for mission work. The fulfillment of this interest arrived in the fall of 1869 when Proft and a group of missionaries departed their European home and sailed for New York.

Proft went on to attend seminary in St. Louis and was ordained and installed as a Lutheran pastor for a Wendish settlement in Fedor, Texas, on September 3, 1871. The same year, he married Dorothea Bertha Elizabeth Koch, but tragedy struck when their first child, an infant daughter, died the following year. Adding to this misery, he lost his wife three days later.

"Proft married again on July 20, 1873, with Dorothea Margaretta Henrietta Stahmer in Washington County, Texas," wrote Robert Proft and George Nielsen for the April 2012 newsletter of the Texas Wendish Historical Society of Serbin, Texas. "An infant son from this marriage died in 1874."

Johann Proft was Wendish and immigrated to the United States, becoming a Lutheran pastor in Texas. Eventually, he received a call to St. John's Lutheran Church in Stringtown and, while living in Missouri, designed two Lutheran churches. *Robert Proft.*

Pastor Proft continued his ministry in Texas for the next several years while he and his wife welcomed three children. During this time, he also supplemented his meager income by continuing his work as a cabinetmaker but was soon called to the ministry in Missouri, the state where he would spend the remainder of this days.

"In 1880, Pastor John A. Proft accepted the call sent him by St. John's [Lutheran Church in Stringtown]," explains the 150th anniversary booklet printed by St. John's in 2017. "During his second year at St. John's, Pastor Proft suffered a great loss [on] April 17, 1882, in the death of his wife….She was given a Christian burial in St. John's Lutheran Church on April 18, 1882."

Robert Proft, great-grandson of the pastor, explained, "Our records show that her last child was stillborn and she passed away two days later."

Later that winter, on December 27, 1882, Pastor Proft was united in marriage in Cole County to his third wife, Maria Magdalena Lehman of Lincoln, Texas.

Referring to the marriage, St. John's historical booklet notes, "Thus the littler children in the Proft home had a mother again, the smallest of the children being Katherine Louise Auguste, who was only one and a half years old when her mother died." The newly married couple would go on to have seven children of their own.

During his tenure at St. John's in Stringtown, Pastor Proft partnered with John Scheperle Sr., a respected member of his congregation and co-owner

In 1882, while Proft was serving as pastor of the St. John's Lutheran Church in Stringtown, his second wife died two days after giving birth to a stillborn child. *Jeremy P. Ämick.*

of the Centennial Mill in Millbrook, to assist another Lutheran church in the area with building a new house of worship.

Proft, whose experience in design included the construction of cabinetry and an altar, created the plans that were used for the second church building at Immanuel Lutheran Church in Honey Creek. The church, which was dedicated in 1884, was built through the oversight of John Scheperle Sr.

Nine years of ministry at St. John's in Stringtown came to a close in 1889 when Proft accepted a call to St. John's Lutheran Church in Corning, Missouri. He again found solace in architecture when he "designed and oversaw the construction of the new brick church in 1893," reported the *St. Joseph News-Press* on July 27, 1985, in an article describing the church's 125th anniversary.

The *Holt County Sentinel*, in its July 24, 1896 edition, reported, "It is a brick building, and we understand the plans were prepared by…Rev. J.A. Proft, who besides being the shepherd of his flock, is an excellent architect."

Yet the husband and father who had endured the loss of two wives and three children began to suffer his own rapid decline in health. This necessitated he resign his position as pastor of St. John's in Corning and move to Lincoln, Missouri. Several weeks later, on December 22, 1896, the fifty-two-year-old Proft died from heart failure and was laid to rest in Zion Lutheran Cemetery in Lincoln. He was survived by his wife, Magdalena, and ten children.

In a life defined by great loss and personal tragedy, Rev. Proft's legacy serves as a testament to his Christian faith. His joyful gifts endure through a stunning monument to his second wife in the cemetery of St. John's Lutheran Church in Stringtown and well-crafted churches in the communities of Honey Creek and Corning.

Well done, good and faithful servant. You have been faithful over a little; I will set you over much. Enter into the joy of your master.
—Matthew 25:21.

CHAPTER 6

TRINITY EVANGELICAL LUTHERAN CHURCH (JEFFERSON CITY)

Helping Unite the Lutherans of the Capital City

T rinity Lutheran Church in Jefferson City shares many historical parallels with the mother of all Lutheran congregations in the area—Zion Lutheran Church. Both congregations have outgrown houses of worship in their early years and have also helped establish other Lutheran congregations in the area. However, where the congregation of Zion Lutheran Church has long since disbanded, Trinity is blessed with a strong ministry that continues to share the Gospel in the local community.

"It was in the year 1869 that a young candidate for the holy ministry, Carl Thurow, was ordained and installed in the Zion Congregation, six miles southwest of Jefferson City," notes the 75th anniversary booklet celebrating the history of Trinity Lutheran Church. "Filled with enthusiasm for the Lord's work, he not only labored zealously in the Zion community, but soon extended his labors into the capital city of the state."

Through Pastor Thurow's support and encouragement, the congregation at Trinity Lutheran church was organized on August 21, 1870. A new church building was then dedicated on a lot on the northeast corner of Monroe and McCarty Streets in downtown Jefferson City.

Prior to this, many of the Lutheran faithful in the Jefferson City area attended services at German Evangelical Central Congregation, now known as Central Church. This mixing of early Lutherans into the congregation at Central Church soon resulted in a legal dispute that was eventually decided by the Missouri Supreme Court.

Trinity Lutheran Church in Jefferson City was organized in 1870 as the Evangelical Lutheran Trinity Church. Pictured is the second church building that was erected in 1895 on the northwest corner of Monroe and McCarty Streets. *Trinity Lutheran, Jefferson City.*

"Christian Routzong was an early German immigrant who settled in the Jefferson City area in the 1830s," said Jack Johnson, a longtime member of Trinity Lutheran Church. "He owned eighty acres of property in Jefferson City and designated a part of the southwest section of that property to be used as a Lutheran cemetery."

In the years prior to the establishment of Trinity Lutheran Church, the cemetery designated by Routzong, now on a triangular section of property between US Highway 54 and South School, became a burial site for Lutherans and those attending the German Evangelical Central Church.

In the years following Routzong's death, trustees of the German Evangelical Central Congregation claimed ownership of the cemetery, maintaining that no Lutheran church existed when Routzong designated the property. The members of the new Trinity Lutheran Church maintained that on August 28, 1852, Routzong deeded the burial ground to the "Lutheran Church" and not Central Church, with whom they held doctrinal differences.

In 1875, less than five years after the organization of Trinity Lutheran Church, the *State Journal* reported in its January 29, 1875 edition that a final judgment was announced by the Missouri Supreme Court: "The judgement rendered in behalf of defendants, and on appropriate decree in conformity with this opinion will be entered here, vesting the title to the property in dispute, in the plaintiffs as trustees of the Evangelical Lutheran Trinity Church, and perpetually enjoining and restraining defendants from further infraction of their rights."

With the matter of cemetery ownership settled in favor of the Lutherans, George Wagner, a member of Central Church, sold a tract of land to be used for the burials of his fellow members of Central Church and all Protestant Germans. Designated the Central Evangelical Cemetery, it was moved in its entirety to Riverview Cemetery between 1964 and 1965 because of the expansion of US Highway 54. Trinity's new church continued to grow on a lot north of the current Jefferson City Police Department. A parsonage was built and, for several years, was where the pastor held classes for the church's parochial school. Due to increasing student enrollment, the parsonage was connected to the church to provide for a classroom.

"Pastor J.H.C. Kaeppel came to the church in 1887 and brought his father with him, who was a trained teacher," Jack Johnson said. "The pastor held morning classes for the students in German, and his father held afternoon classes in English." Johnson added, "Because his father was a trained teacher, the enrollment doubled in the parochial school from thirty to sixty students."

The year following Pastor Kaeppel's arrival, Trinity Lutheran Church became a member of the Lutheran Church–Missouri Synod.

"In the meantime, the congregation was growing rapidly," explains Trinity's 75th anniversary booklet. "March 3, 1895, [the congregation] resolved to purchase the property across the street from the church on the northwest

corner of Monroe and McCarty Streets. On
that site a new church was built and formally
dedicated to God's service in November 1895."

"We refer to the 1895 church as the 'steeple
church,' and it sits where the Missouri Bar
Association building is now located," Jack
Johnson explained.

In 1922, the decision was made to purchase for
$25,000 the former Central Public School, which
would help accommodate exceptional growth in
the parochial school. The school building was
situated alongside the brick home that became
the new parsonage. Both the parsonage and
the Central Public School no longer exist but
stood on the property of what has become the
DoubleTree Hotel on Monroe Street.

By the late 1920s, Word War I was several
years in hindsight; however, church history notes
that use of the German language in worship services remained a concern.

Pastor J.H.C. Kaeppel was installed at Trinity in 1897 and also taught classes in the parochial school. *Trinity Lutheran, Jefferson City.*

"Continuing German services made it difficult to witness to the English-speaking people in town as well as the trust issue [from the country being involved in a war with Germany]," describes the booklet from 2020 commemorating Trinity's 150th anniversary. "English services were added to Sunday morning worship at 9:45, and German remained at 11:00." The book further explains, "It was hard for the congregation to break with its German heritage."

When the United States entered World War II in December 1941, Trinity Lutheran Church in Jefferson City had recently turned seventy-one years old. This soon became a transformative period for the church founded by German immigrants, now witnessing many of its congregation members entering into a war with the very country where their recent ancestors were born.

"During World War II, there was a USO near the church, and many of the soldiers would come to worship services on Sunday mornings," said Bethel Johnson, who, along with her husband, Jack, is a Trinity Lutheran Church historian.

"Since many of these servicemen had friends fighting against German forces overseas or they could themselves be deployed, the decision was made to hold the services entirely in English instead of German," Johnson added.

In 1943, the church's assistant pastor, Wallace Allen Pohl, made the decision to enlist in the U.S. Army and served as a chaplain. After the war, he became pastor of a Lutheran church in Milwaukee but, sadly, died from a heart attack in 1958 at only forty-five years old.

The years after the war also resulted in extraordinary growth and an opportunity for the members of Trinity to help plant a new Lutheran congregation in the Jefferson City community.

"Starting a new congregation is not a decision made quickly," explains Trinity's 125th anniversary booklet. "The district sent a representative [in 1949] to assess Jefferson City as to its potential to sustain a second congregation. The assessment covered the last twenty years for population growth, ethnic diversity, industrial and economic growth, [and] transportation."

With the Western District of the Lutheran Church—Missouri Synod submitting a recommendation in support of the proposal, a new congregation was established as Faith Evangelical Lutheran Church on April 11, 1950, with the seed of 199 members from Trinity. Despite the loss of members of Trinity's congregation in order to organize Faith Lutheran, both churches quickly flourished. Soon, the members of Trinity agreed that they had outgrown their facilities downtown and began the search for a new location for their church and parochial school.

"They purchased thirteen acres of property on Swifts Highway that used to be the gardens owned by Henry Schmidt and George Walther," said

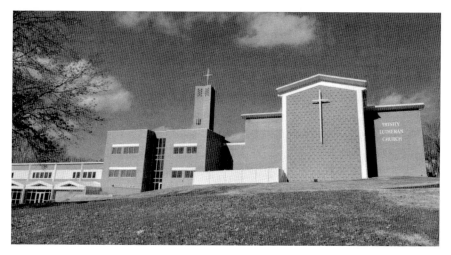

The new Trinity Lutheran Church was dedicated at its current location on April 23, 1961, with 1,600 people in attendance. *Trinity Lutheran Church.*

Jack Johnson. "They were Lutherans who had used the property to raise vegetables they sold around Jefferson City."

Groundbreaking for the new church, school and parsonage occurred on November 8, 1959, and the cornerstone was set five days later. The construction contract was for $640,000 with an additional allotment of $140,300 for furnishings, parking lots, landscaping and the parsonage. The dedication for the new church complex was held on April 23, 1961, and attended by a crowd estimated at 1,600.

The church and associated structures were built by the Roy Scheperle Construction Company. The company's namesake, Roy Scheperle, was the great-nephew of John Scheperle Sr., who built Immanuel Lutheran Church in Honey Creek in 1884 and St. John's Lutheran Church in Stringtown in 1905.

"I can remember when we moved into the new school; it was quite the experience," recalled Bethel Johnson. "The teachers, staff and students

The groundbreaking for the new Trinity Lutheran Church and school on Swifts Highway took place on November 8, 1959. *Trinity Lutheran Church.*

gathered all of their books and supplies and walked from the old school on Monroe Street to the new school by the church on Swifts Highway."

Bethel Johnson also explained that there is a round communion window in the back of the current sanctuary that was salvaged from behind the altar of the 1895 church when it was demolished. There is also a series of stained-glass windows in the upper section of the church designed by Ernoe Koch and manufactured by Jacoby Studios in St. Louis. She continued, "Each window tells a specific story related to our faith, and they all are part of a theme known as Rivers of Life, and it flows from the Great Trinity window."

When the church moved to its current location, the property contained a historic house known as the Porth Mansion. For many years, this structure was used for several purposes, but it eventually fell into disrepair and was demolished.

A few years later, after the new church was dedicated, another interesting historical moment unfolded involving the church cemetery. During the mid-1960s, a major construction project was underway to expand US Highway 54 through Jefferson City. A section of the Trinity Lutheran Church Cemetery was in the path of the new highway, so there were many graves that had to be exhumed and relocated.

"The section of the cemetery that was moved was where they had buried members of the Central Church decades ago," said Jack Johnson. "Those bodies were taken to Riverview Cemetery and reinterred there."

Trustees of Trinity Lutheran Church continue to maintain the cemetery, which, according to church records, contains 167 marked graves and a little more than a dozen that are unmarked.

Since Jack and Bethel Johnson became the second couple married in the new church in 1961, it has undergone many expansions and witnessed both spiritual and physical growth. In light of all these changes, the couple strives to preserve the church's fascinating legacy as has been done by generations before them.

"The first and second church have been gone for many decades along with the school and parsonage that was on Monroe Street," Bethel said. "A lot of the tangible history of the church has disappeared." She added, "But the people throughout Trinity's history have been devout and truly family-oriented, seeking to share their faith with their children and community while also providing for a good education. These are all traditions that continue with the congregation."

CHAPTER 7

IMMANUEL LUTHERAN CHURCH

(HONEY CREEK)

Springing Forth from the Influence of Zion

S everal miles south of Jefferson City lies an unincorporated community named for a stream that flows into the Moreau River. Honey Creek, which received its name from early settlers impressed by the many beehives found in the area, was soon settled by German immigrants who not only began to farm the area but also established a Lutheran church shortly after the Civil War. In July 1843, Zion Lutheran Church was organized near Jefferson City, becoming the mother church for many congregations in Cole County, such as St. Paul's Lutheran Church in Lohman, St. John's Lutheran Church in Stringtown and Trinity Lutheran Church in Jefferson City.

Immanuel Lutheran Church was officially established on August 29, 1870, through the efforts of "Lutheran families living in the Honey Creek vicinity [who] had formed one congregation with the Lutheran Zion Church…from 1850 until the organization of the Honey Creek Church," reported the *Jefferson City Post-Tribune* on July 25, 1930. This organizational effort included a significant amount of involvement from Pastor Carl Thurow of Zion Lutheran Church, who not only supported several Lutheran congregations in Cole County but also had recently helped organize Trinity Lutheran Church in Jefferson City, as described in the previous chapter.

The first church was a one-room log structure built in 1868 on land donated by John Duenckel, a charter church member. Prior to this, circuit pastors traveling on horseback from Zion Lutheran Church provided spiritual leadership for several area congregations. In 1870, Immanuel Lutheran Church of Honey Creek welcomed its first full-time pastor, Rev. Conrad Vetter.

Organized in 1870 in the community of Honey Creek, Immanuel Lutheran Church has remained a vibrant congregation throughout the decades. Pictured is the second church, which was dedicated in 1884. *Immanuel Lutheran Church.*

According to a historical booklet printed for Immanuel Lutheran's 150th anniversary, Pastor Vetter was "promised a salary of $200 a year plus 50 cents for each child in school. In addition, each member would provide 50 pounds of flour per year…[and] free housing would also be provided."

Conrad Vetter became the first full-time pastor of Immanuel Lutheran Church in 1870. The German native was seventy-three years old when he died in 1907. *Immanuel Lutheran Church.*

Pastor Vetter not only led his congregation but also taught at the parochial school that had been established in 1868. In 1872, a parsonage was built for the pastor and his family. Sadly, during his thirteen-year term at Honey Creek, two of Pastor Vetter's children died and were interred in the newly established church cemetery.

Shortly before Pastor Vetter departed Honey Creek, a new church building was proposed. The design for the church was drawn by Pastor John A. Proft of St. John's Lutheran Church in Stringtown. Pastor Proft later accepted a call to St. John's Lutheran Church in Corning, Missouri, helping design a new church for that congregation as well.

The new Immanuel Lutheran Church was built by St. John's Lutheran Church (Stringtown) member John Scheperle Sr., co-owner of the Centennial Mill in Millbrook. Years later, Scheperle Sr. would serve as the contractor for the new St. John's Lutheran Church in Stringtown that was dedicated in 1905.

Pastor Vetter departed Immanuel in 1883, and the new Immanuel Lutheran Church was dedicated the following year. The original log church was moved a short distance to the west, reduced in size and utilized as a school until 1924.

A church history booklet explains, "In 1917 the congregation voted to preach in the English language for the first time, but only once every six or eight weeks." It further notes, "By 1936, half of the services were held in English and half in German."

"In 1924, a modern school building was erected by the congregation," reported the *Sunday News and Tribune* on September 2, 1945. "The pastors of the church served as teachers until 1928, when members of the church engaged teachers to carry on the education of their children."

"Church records show that our old altar came from the former St. Aloysius Catholic Church [near Osage Bluff] sometime around 1880," said longtime Immanuel member Schellie Blochberger. "We used it for several decades, but it has since been donated to Grace Lutheran Church in Holts Summit," she added.

The congregation at Immanuel voted to join the Missouri Synod in 1888 and welcomed many dedicated and competent pastors throughout the next several years. Notable on this list is Ernst Bultmann, who served Immanuel from 1913 to 1946, the longest-serving pastor to date, and who helped usher the congregation through the tumultuous periods of both World Wars. After his thirty-three-year stint with Immanuel Lutheran Church, Pastor Bultmann was granted a release by the congregation so that he could accept a call to Holy Cross Lutheran Church in Lake Creek, Missouri. Bultmann retired from the ministry in 1949 and returned to the Jefferson City area to live out the remainder of his days. He was seventy-eight years of age when he died on September 28, 1961, and was laid to rest in the cemetery of Immanuel Lutheran Church.

During World War II, members of the congregation raised money for the war effort, and twenty-five young men from the congregation served in the military, all of whom returned home. A respectable number of updates were made to the church and parsonage as the years passed, including the installation of electrical and water systems. A new basement was excavated beneath the church in 1945, and classrooms were later added to the school.

A native of Wisconsin and a U.S. Army veteran who served in the Korean War, Pastor Ervin Junkans came to serve the congregation of Immanuel Lutheran Church in the late 1960s. Although he went on to serve other Lutheran congregations in other states, Junkans retired to the Jefferson City area in 1996 and continued to serve as an interim pastor for several local Lutheran churches. He maintained membership at St. John's Lutheran Church in Schubert and, after his passing in 2011, was laid to rest in the church cemetery. His son, Paul Junkans, became a charter member of Our Savior's Lutheran Church, which is discussed in an upcoming chapter.

An anniversary booklet confirms, "In the fall of 1976, the multipurpose building was built and the Fall Festival was held for the first time the following year." It adds, "In the summer of 1979, $20,000 was spent to redecorate and repair the church (rebuilding of the steeple, tuckpointing, waterproofing, painting and decorating inside)."

Eventually, following the installation of Pastor Jeffrey Schanbacher in 2009, a new church and school were completed. More recently, the school gymnasium has undergone a complete renovation.

The Missouri Synod congregation, which organized with between eight to ten people in 1870, has grown to more than six hundred confirmed members. Most of the original church structures have since been replaced, and worship services are now conducted entirely in English, but the

Left: Pastor Ernst Bultmann was installed at Immanuel Lutheran Church on November 8, 1913, and served the congregation of Honey Creek for thirty-three years. *Immanuel Lutheran Church.*

Right: Pastor Ervin Junkans was installed at Immanuel Lutheran Church on November 3, 1968. One of his sons went on to become a charter member of Peace Lutheran Church in the 1980s. *Immanuel Lutheran Church.*

congregation's dedication to their Christian faith and preservation of Immanuel's history remains.

"We had a former member who was instrumental in getting the old German records that included marriages, deaths and baptisms translated into English," said Schellie Blochberger. "This, along with previous church histories, allowed us to compile a substantial historical record for the church's 150th anniversary in 2020." She added, "Many of the original families who established the church or those who were early members still have descendants in the Honey Creek area—many of these families are still connected to the church."

In conclusion, Blochberger noted that the church continues to share the message of its original constitution and bylaws, by striving "to foster Christian fellowship and love [and] to extend a helping hand in human needs."

CHAPTER 8

OSAGE BLUFF METHODIST CHURCH

A Congregation with Ties to Zion Lutheran Church

The beginnings of Osage Bluff Methodist Church date to 1842, when Sebastian Barth, a circuit-riding preacher and missionary, was sent to Missouri by the American Tract Society. Author Nathan Bangs, describing the society in *The Reviewer Answered* (1830), notes: "In addition to the direct influence which this society exerts upon the public sentiment by the circulation of its tracts, some of which are no inconsiderable volumes, it exerts a mighty influence by the labors of its agents, every one of whom is a missionary to all intents and purposes, thought deriving his support from the funds of the American Tract Society."

Barth came to Pennsylvania from Hesse, Germany, with his parents in the early 1830s. More than a decade later, in 1843, he embraced the support provided by the American Tract Society to answer the call to establish German Methodist congregations in Missouri communities such as Lake Creek near Smithton, Jamestown, Pilot, Boonville and Lexington. He traveled by horseback, often accompanied by H. Nuelson and under the earthly authority of Rev. Ludwig Jacoby of St. Louis, the latter of whom had become a Lutheran pastor in Germany but joined the Methodist Church after his arrival in America. At the time of Barth's missionary assignment, Jacoby was serving in his appointed role of supervisor of the mission work for German-speaking people in the region.

The coming years bore witness to the great lengths to which Barth went in establishing German Methodism as part of the Osage Mission, which stretched from the Osage River south of Jefferson City some 150 miles

The Osage Bluff Methodist Church was established in 1865. Pictured is the second church building used by the congregation. *Friedens Church Brazito.*

distance to the vicinity of the community of Lexington. This work resulted in the planting of four parishes in Cole County that included Bethel Church, seven miles southwest of Jefferson City; Union Church, a few miles east of California; a third church near Taos; and a fourth in Jefferson City. Some of these parishes died out over the next several years, but several of their congregation members chose to establish a new church five miles west of the Moreau.

In the 1906 book *Jubiläumsbuch der St. Louis Deutschen Konferenz* (*Anniversary Book of the St. Louis German Conference*), it is noted that Osage Bluff Church came into existence on October 12, 1865, when a group met at the site where the first church building would be erected five years later. Situated along what is now Route E between Brazito and Osage Bluff, the Osage Bluff Methodist Church came into existence with its first church building resembling many of the early church structures that were cut from the wilderness and constructed from logs. A new frame-structure church was erected in 1899 under the guidance of its pastor, John P. Koeller. The dedication of the new church took place on October 29, 1899, at which time William Crede and John Engelbrecht Sr. were trustees while Luis Bachman and Chris Engelbrecht were stewards. Many of these surnames were associated with Immanuel Lutheran Church in Honey Creek and, within the next four years, Friedens Church in Brazito.

According to the *Northwestern Christian Advocate* (a publication of the Methodist Church) in its booklet dated August 30, 1905, Koeller had by that time left the Osage Bluff Methodist Church and moved to St. Louis. Prior to this move, he had also pastored at the German Methodist Church in Jefferson City. After moving to St. Louis, he was associated with the St. Louis Conference and was "chosen principal of Enterprise Normal Academy… the conference seminary" in Enterprise, Kansas. The booklet further describes the clergyman: "He is thirty-six years old, and a graduate of Central Wesleyan College, Warrenton, Mo." On October 17, 1899, Koeller married Helen Nuelsen in St. Louis and later moved to Wisconsin, where he was pastor of Methodist churches and raised two sons and a daughter. The September 9, 1957 edition of the *Oshkosh Northwestern* explained that Rev. Koeller was eighty-seven years old when he passed away on September 9, 1957, and is interred in Lake View Memorial Park in Oshkosh, Wisconsin, alongside his wife, who preceded him in death by two years.

The congregation of this church began to dwindle in the following years, and many members chose to join some of their fellow Germans attending the Lutheran Church in nearby Honey Creek or the German Evangelical Church in Brazito. By the late 1940s, the decision was made to close the church, and the building was sold to the church in Brazito for use as a fellowship hall. All that now remains on the site of the former church is a cemetery with a few dozen graves.

There are many potential reasons why many German immigrants embraced the Methodist church at a time when they were hemmed in by German Evangelical and German Lutheran congregations. Some historians

After the Osage Bluff Methodist Church closed, the building was moved to Brazito and installed on the back of Friedens Church, where it continues to be used as a fellowship hall. *Friedens Church Brazito.*

believe that many of these immigrants no longer wished to retain the distinctive characteristics of their homeland but instead sought to leave behind the German language services and embrace other denominations, such as the Methodist church, whose members were utilizing the English language and pursuing recognition as Americans. Others simply grew displeased with the disunity in the early Lutheran Church in the United States, finding that German Methodist congregations offered them the opportunity to unify with those of their homeland in worship that comported with their individual doctrinal viewpoints.

The Koch Family

The congregation at Osage Bluff Methodist Church boasts many interesting historical characters, such as one of its founding members, Johann Peter Koch. Born on February 8, 1809, in the vicinity of Munich, Germany, he was one of the many early German immigrants who landed at the port in New Orleans and traveled up the Mississippi River before eventually settling in central Missouri. He lost his first wife shortly after coming to the United States, being left to raise a daughter, Catherine. He again found companionship in another German native, Barbara Engelbrecht, whom he married in Jefferson City and with whom he raised two daughters and a son. Records indicate that prior to settling in the community of Osage Bluff, he was among the thirty-seven founding members of Zion Lutheran Church, mentioned in the first chapter. The family would eventually settle on a farm in the Osage Bluff area and help establish the Methodist church that carried the name of the nearly forgotten community.

According to one interesting story, Johann was a member of the Cole County Home Guard during the Civil War, which is verified by his service card that reveals he enlisted on June 19, 1861, when he was fifty-two years of age. An article titled "Life of a Home Guard and Enrolled Missouri Militia" on a Civil War historical website explains, "Created in the summer of 1861 by General Nathaniel Lyon, the Home Guard were supposed to stay at home and go into action only to defend their neighborhoods."

Additionally, the men in these companies were not issued uniforms and often had to utilize their own weapons. Although they were neither traveling under the flags of Union generals nor engaged in direct combat on faraway battlefields against Confederate forces, this did not remove them from the dangers present in the Missouri backwoods during the Civil War.

"[Johann Koch] was building a new house on his farm near Osage Bluff and was working on the roof when General [Sterling] Price came along with his army and took him prisoner, holding him in captivity for some time," explains Carrie Westlake Whitney in *Kansas City, Missouri: Its History and Its People, 1800–1908*. "He was a staunch supporter of the Union cause and it was because of his sympathy with the Federal government that the Confederate general held him a captive until exchanged."

The elder Koch remained engaged in farming and was seventy-eight years old when he died on June 11, 1887. On his passing, he was laid to rest in the cemetery outside of the Osage Bluff Methodist Church, which he had helped organize several years earlier. His second wife, Barbara, died less than two years later and was interred alongside him.

Johann's son, Henry Koch, was born on October 3, 1851, near Osage Bluff. As an only son, Henry grew into adulthood working on the farm and, demonstrating his educational leanings, later teaching school for many years in rural Cole County. In 1875, he married Margaretha Steininger from Osage City, who was the daughter of a German immigrant. Furthermore, since his father was a convert to the German Methodist faith, the younger Koch began his own association with the church. Henry Koch and his wife for many years lived and worked the farm established by his father. He became a member of the Osage Bluff Methodist Church in 1871 and served in many church offices, including that of Sunday school leader. His parents' farm he later sold, purchasing new farmland near Jefferson City and later choosing to embark on mercantile endeavors by purchasing a grocery store in the same city. Then, in 1887, he moved his family to Kansas City after he purchased a grocery store there, which he operated until his passing on April 1, 1894, when he was only forty-two years old. He was laid to rest in Forest Hill Cemetery in Kansas City.

CHAPTER 9

GERMAN EVANGELICAL EMANUEL LUTHERAN CHURCH (CENTERTOWN)

A Near Forgotten Lutheran Congregation Remembered by a Small Cemetery

The German Evangelical Emanuel Lutheran Church was once located in Centertown and possessed simplistic, yet stunning, architectural features that were preserved through a painting created by the late Hazel A. Andtwiler. This painting was done in the 1950s but reveals the church as it appeared around 1900. The church was established in 1876, and on August 25, 1877, the adjoining property was purchased to be used as the church cemetery, although records indicate the first burial occurred as early as 1871. With the property that included the cemetery, the church sat on nearly three acres.

An early member of the church, John Frederick Flessa, was a native of Bavaria and founded and operated the Flessa Flouring Mills in Centertown with his son, John Jacob. In later years, John Jacob embarked on his own career in carpentry and eventually ended up working for the railroad. In 1900, the family patriarch, John F. Flessa, partnered with other investors to found the Centertown Milling Company—an endeavor that included Bailey Lansdown, a successful business owner from Russellville who moved to Centertown the same year the mill was established, opening the Lansdown Mercantile Company. Both John F. Flessa and his wife, Eva, are buried in the cemetery along with their son John Jacob. One of Flessa's sons, Adam, came of age and was confirmed in the Lutheran church in Centertown while also assisting his father in the management of the milling operation in Centertown. He later helped manage a mill near Russellville and managed the Russellville livery stable prior to his retirement in 1948. After marrying

The German Evangelical Emanuel Lutheran Church was established in Centertown in 1876. All that remains of the church is a cemetery off Lookout Trail. *Hazel Andtwiler.*

Viola Campbell in 1896, he joined Cole Spring Baptist Church in Russellville and was buried in Enloe Cemetery following his death in 1956.

Another partner to Flessa in the Centertown Milling Company endeavor was John Leonard Blochberger, another Bavarian immigrant who also helped found the Lutheran church in Centertown. Blochberger was heavily involved in agriculture and operated a farm north of Centertown; one of his sons, William, went on to own successful businesses in locations such as Lohman, Cole Camp and Sedalia. Another interesting historical connection is that when John L. Blochberger was twenty-five years old in 1852, several German immigrants met in the home of his father, Johann Adam Plochberger (the *P* and *B* in the name are often interchanged during this period in Lohman-area history) to establish what became St. Paul's Evangelical Lutheran Church in Lohman.

With the small congregation at the German Evangelical Emanuel Lutheran Church unable to support a full-time pastor, for many years, it had to lean on the generous nature of fellow Lutheran congregations. For a number of years, Pastor George Fikenscher from St. Paul's Lutheran Church in Lohman provided services for the small Centertown congregation, but in 1891, he made the decision to suspend his services there and focus on his primary calling at Lohman. It was then that the Centertown congregation reached out to St. John's Lutheran Church in Schubert near Taos, requesting that they provide the clerical support the congregation was so desperately seeking.

"A delegation from Immanuel Church, Centertown, appeared at the January 1, 1892 meeting to request that Pastor (Ernest Frederick) Geyer [pastor of St. John's Lutheran Church in Schubert] hold services in their parish once a month," explains the booklet *A History of St. John's Lutheran Church—Schubert*. "After a lively debate, the request was granted by a small majority vote, for a term of one year. A year later, the Centertown parish sent Pastor Geyer a regular call, asking that he come to them every three weeks and on the 'second holydays' [Pentecost Monday, Easter Monday, Second Christmas Day]. On those days, St. John's was to have the afternoon services. Reluctantly, St. John's agreed to the arrangement."

In 1895, when the new congregation at Trinity Evangelical Lutheran Church in Russellville was established, Pastor J. Paul Franke, who was pastor at St. Paul's Lutheran Church in the nearby Moniteau County community of California, also began serving the fledgling congregation at Russellville. Pastor Franke volunteered to fill in at Centertown as well during times when Pastor Geyer was not available. In late 1897, a special meeting was held at St. John's Lutheran Church in Schubert and the proposal made to cancel the dual-parish arrangement as supported by Pastor Geyer from St. John's in Schubert. The decision was made to allow Pastor Geyer to continue supporting the Centertown congregation until Easter 1898.

When Pastor Franke accepted another call in 1897 and moved to Topeka, Kansas, he was succeeded at Trinity Lutheran Church in Russellville

Pastor Alfred Finkbeiner was pastor of St. John's Lutheran Church in Schubert from 1912 to 1916. He became the second-to-last pastor to fulfill the dual-parish role with the church in Centertown. *St. John's Lutheran Church, Schubert.*

The Reverend O. Rossbach served as pastor of Trinity Lutheran Church in Russellville from 1923 to 1944, while also supporting the Lutheran church in Centertown. *Trinity Lutheran, Russellville.*

by Pastor F. Schardt, who also lived in California but served the circuit consisting of the three churches in California, Russellville and Centertown. During a meeting at Trinity in Russellville on July 9, 1899, "the congregation voted to extend a call to Pastor Schardt to move to Russellville and serve California and Centertown from here. This arrangement was accepted by the pastor, and work was begun on the construction of a parsonage....Late in the fall of 1899 the parsonage was dedicated and the Schardt family established residence there." In the spring of 1905, Pastor Schardt accepted a call to a new congregation in Nebraska, and it appears this is the time that the church in Centertown began experiencing significant problems in finding a pastor to support regular services for its own church family.

The next several years would see St. John's Lutheran Church in Schubert continue to provide pastoral support to fellow Lutherans in Centertown. A native of Switzerland, Pastor Alfred Finkbeiner was installed at St. John's in 1912, and he abided by the dual-parish agreement that had been in place prior to his arrival. He continued to support both congregations until accepting a call to Wakeeny, Kansas, in late January 1916. He was succeeded by Pastor Ernst Kaatz, who faithfully served both congregations until his departure in 1919. After he left St. John's in Schubert, the congregation entered into membership in the Missouri Synod while Emanuel in Centertown began its decline.

Despite waning membership, the congregation was served by Pastor O. Rossbach of Trinity Lutheran Church in Russellville from 1923 to 1944. After Pastor Rossbach departed and his support to the Centertown church also ended, Pastor W.H. Schwab from St. Paul's Lutheran Church in California, a Missouri Synod pastor, provided ministerial support for approximately six months until such time as regular church services were suspended due to poor attendance. The congregation soon disbanded, and the former church building fell into a state of deterioration because of both age and vandalism. The building was sold to the highest bidder in the early 1960s, and the ninety dollars collected following its demolition went into a fund to support the cemetery. The cemetery remains a visible reminder of this once-thriving congregation, and at certain times of the year, one can still see evidence of the outline of the limestone block foundation of the former church building. The front of the church building faced north toward Lookout Trail (Old Highway 50); the road passing by the left (east) side of the church is North Waterford.

Records indicate that the bell from the belfry of the church in Centertown went to Our Savior's Lutheran Church in Jefferson City in 1960 as a gift from Centertown Church's sole remaining members, Otto and Edith Schramm. Both Otto and his wife are interred in the Lutheran cemetery at Centertown. Since October 1977, St. Paul's Lutheran Church in California has assumed responsibility for the care and maintenance of the cemetery.

There are several familiar surnames connected to Centertown, Schubert, Stringtown, Millbrook, Lohman, Russellville and other surrounding communities that one may identify on a stroll through this near-forgotten cemetery. For a number of years, local residents Hilbert and Wanda Strobel helped care for it by coordinating such activities as resetting a number of fallen grave markers. Hilbert was a lifelong member of St. Paul's Lutheran Church in California, but when he passed away in 2012, he was laid to rest in the Evangelical Lutheran Emanuel Cemetery in Centertown. His wife, the former Wanda Blumhost, passed away in 2020 and was laid to rest alongside him in the cemetery they lovingly helped maintain for a number of years.

CHAPTER 10

TRINITY EVANGELICAL LUTHERAN CHURCH (RUSSELLVILLE)

Congregation Built through Dedication of German Immigrant Entrepreneurs

A s many immigrants from various regions of Germany began to settle in the Russellville area prior to the beginning of the twentieth century, they generally had two options with regard to maintaining their connection to the Lutheran faith of their homeland— travel a good distance by horseback to locations such as Lohman, Centertown or California, all of which were several miles' distance, or forego attending worship services altogether. Neither option was viewed as being acceptable in the eyes of visionaries such as John Jacob Buchta and Michael Schubert.

In 1895, John J. Buchta and Michael Schubert, both of German descent and actively engaged in business endeavors in the Russellville area, began the work of organizing a Lutheran church. With scores of German immigrants and their descendants having already established Lutheran churches in nearby communities such as Lohman and Stringtown, these trustees sought to form a new house of worship, one that would soon become a centerpiece of community involvement in Russellville. It was through their dedicated leadership, hard work and financial support that this became a reality.

"Pastor [Paul] Franke conducted services September 1, 1895, although the congregation was not yet fully organized," wrote Dr. Roger Jungmeyer, a professor of history at Lincoln University, in an application for inclusion of the church on the National Register of Historic Places. Dr. Jungmeyer added, "During the same time Trinity at Russellville was being organized [Pastor Franke] was serving a church at California, Missouri."

The second—and current—church building for Trinity Lutheran Church in Russellville was dedicated on August 4, 1912, nearly seventeen years after it was first established. *Trinity Lutheran, Russellville.*

A congregation began to assemble, with church records revealing that the first funeral and burial were conducted on October 28, 1895, followed by the first baptism on November 3, 1895. A one-acre plot of land was purchased on the west side of Marion Street in Russellville, where a small frame church and a parsonage were erected. The first church cost $640 to erect; however, no pictures of this structure have been located. Based on records maintained by Pastor J. Paul Franke, the first church was dedicated on September 13, 1896, and was celebrated by two services: a morning worship service conducted in German and an afternoon service in English.

Pastor Franke, at the time of his assisting in the establishment of Trinity Lutheran Church in Russellville, had been serving as pastor of St. Paul's Lutheran Church in the Moniteau County community of California in addition to conducting occasional worship services at the Lutheran church in Centertown. In 1897, Pastor Franke, who was himself a German immigrant, left the congregation in Russellville and went on to serve Lutheran congregations in the St. Louis area, Illinois and Nebraska. The *Albion Argus* reported on August 8, 1918, that the forty-nine-year-old Franke, his wife and their two daughters were killed on July 29, 1918, when the car they were traveling in was struck by a train while crossing tracks in Marshall County, Iowa. The family was laid to rest in New Bethlehem Memorial Park Cemetery in St. Louis County, Missouri.

Michael Schubert and John Jacob Buchta, on behalf of the growing congregation that had been kick-started by Pastor Franke, acquired two acres of land south of Russellville on September 12, 1896, and established the church cemetery. Frederick Schardt and Charles Schober would later serve the congregation as pastors, but it was under the guidance of Rev. C. Schaff, who received his call to Trinity in 1910, that the congregation's arc of growth continued unabated.

John Jacob Buchta, a German immigrant, became one of the organizing members of Trinity Lutheran Church in 1895. *Don and Roger Buchta.*

"In 1911, an opportunity presented itself to sell the old church property for $2,500.00," noted a "Historical Sketch" featured in the church's Golden Jubilee booklet from 1945. "On March 26, this offer was accepted. Steps were immediately taken to build first the parsonage on the new ground [its current location]…with eight rooms and a solid brick structure costing the congregation the sum of $1,900.00."

The parsonage was dedicated in early October 1911, and only a few days later, the cornerstone was laid for the new church building. The brick church, measuring thirty-six by seventy feet and featuring two spires, was dedicated on August 4, 1912. The church was situated just east of the parsonage, its front facing the unpaved "Old Versailles Road" (now State Highway C). It was on May 21, 1914, that the congregation at Trinity Lutheran Church officially incorporated. Three years later, on July 15, 1917, the church chose to affiliate with the Iowa Synod, just as their sister congregation at St. Paul's Lutheran Church in Lohman had done decades earlier. Although much interesting synodical history unfolded in the intervening years, the Iowa Synod underwent a merger to form the American Lutheran Church, which has since become the Evangelical Lutheran Church of America (ELCA). To this day, Trinity Lutheran Church and St. Paul's maintain affiliation with the ELCA.

A white one-room schoolhouse was dedicated in 1912 and used for confirmation classes for a number of years; however, it has more recently been utilized as an office and meeting space and for storage. The schoolhouse would also be used for several years by the Russellville School District prior to the construction of additional classrooms on the nearby school campus.

Another important period in the early history of the church began on July 4, 1923. It was on this date that Rev. F. Otto Rossbach "from Stuttgart, Kansas, assumed the ministry of the congregation," explained the church's seventy-fifth anniversary booklet from 1970. "Two important personal events during the time of his pastorate were his marriage to Miss Hattie Schlutz on October 29, 1924, and the ordination of his son Walter (a child from a previous marriage) in 1938."

Rev. Rossbach earned the distinction of being the longest-serving pastor for Trinity Lutheran church in Russellville, serving the congregation from 1923 to 1944. During World War II, his son Walter volunteered as a chaplain in the Canadian army. During his time with the Russellville congregation, Pastor Rossbach also provided ministerial support to the Lutheran congregation in Centertown on an occasional basis since they did not have the resources to support a full-time pastor because of declining membership.

Michael Schubert and John Jacob Buchta, on behalf of the growing congregation at Trinity, acquired two acres of land south of Russellville on September 12, 1896, and established the church cemetery. *Jeremy P. Ämick.*

The seventy-eight-year-old Rev. Rossbach passed away in 1948 and was laid to rest in Saint Peter Cemetery in New Richland, Minnesota. On May 11, 1940, during Rossbach's tenure at Trinity, the parish hall was dedicated on land donated by the widow of Michael Schubert, whose husband helped organize the church decades earlier. Initially, the hall measured thirty-six by seventy-four feet with an auditorium and full basement. Years later, classrooms and storage were added to the south side of the parish hall.

Rev. John J. Haberaecker, who had previously served in the Kansas City area, accepted a call to serve the congregation and was installed on June 10, 1945. The church celebrated its fiftieth anniversary with a Golden Jubilee service held on Sunday, November 11, 1945. Two celebratory services were held that day under the guidance of Rev. Erwin Fritschel, president of the Central District of the American Lutheran Church, and Rev. Johannes Lehmann, president emeritus of the Central District.

Church records reveal a number of changes made during Rev. Haberaecker's ministry, including the complete transition to English-language worship services, while the long-embraced German-language services were reserved for special occasions.

"At a congregational meeting in July 1955, plans were approved for a rock veneer building in the cemetery to be used for storage and shelter; a rock entrance to the cemetery and shrubbery had been added earlier," explains the seventy-fifth anniversary booklet.

Due to illness, Haberaecker's sixteen-year ministry ended in 1961, and the next two decades witnessed the spiritual leadership of Revs. Robert G. Wessels, Harold Martens and Howard Ellis. During the seventy-fifth anniversary worship service held on August 16, 1970, Rev. Walter Rossbach, whose father had served as pastor more than a quarter century earlier, conducted a special service honoring the church's longevity.

The last few decades have witnessed many improvements made to the church and parish hall, restoration of the schoolhouse and the construction of a garage and pavilion. In 2020, the church celebrated its 125th anniversary and, through the research and dedication of Dr. Roger Jungmeyer, has earned designation as a historic district on the National Register of Historic Places.

The church turned to the late Erna Raithel, a longtime congregation member and pillar of the community, for the words that best describe the blessings that Trinity Lutheran Church has both given and received during its years of ministry: "May Trinity in the coming years continue to be a blessing to its members and to the community of which it is a part; may

A one-room schoolhouse was constructed behind the church in 1912. This schoolhouse still stands and has been used as an office and a meeting space and for storage. *Jeremy P. Ämick.*

Trinity continue to be loyal and devoted to carrying out the commands of its loving Savior; and may Trinity always express praise and Thanksgiving to our faithful God."

ADAM JAHREIS

Adam Jahreis was a man who, like so many of his fellow Lutherans in the Russellville area, had an interesting story beginning in his German homeland. Following his immigration to the United States, he married a widow with whom he raised several children and embraced opportunities to raise them up in the ways of Christian fellowship.

Born on July 9, 1873, at Muenchberg in Bavaria, a community that has since become a partner city to Jefferson City, Adam Jahreis later attended a local school with Christian instruction and was confirmed in his family's Lutheran faith in 1886, just shy of his thirteenth birthday. Since he was considered an able-bodied young man, the Bavarian Army Reform of 1868 necessitated that he both train and serve for three years with the Bavarian army before embarking on his own interests.

"Adam was my grandfather, and our family records show that he came to the United States in early 1897, when he was still twenty-three years old," said Candace Stockton. "He was accompanied by Henry Raithel (who established a farm on Branch Road between Russellville and Lohman) and Carl Wolfrum. The story our family has shared is that when Adam and Henry brought Carl Wolfrum with them from Germany, he was only nine or ten years old. Apparently, his parents were very poor, had several children and couldn't afford to feed them all. My grandfather and Henry essentially took care of Carl until he was an adult."

Finding many Germans in the area, Jahreis settled near Russellville and, in April 1899, married the widow Rosina (Jungmeyer) Schmoeger. At the time, she had one son, William Schmoeger, whose father, Frederick, died a few years earlier. Together, Jahreis and his new bride raised William and later added to the family four daughters—Bertha, Hulda, Ruth and Anna.

Adam Jahreis immigrated to the Russellville area from Bavaria in 1897. He married Rosina Schmoeger, a local widow who had been left with a son to raise. Jahreis farmed in Russellville and raised his children in the Lutheran faith. *Candace Stockton.*

Church records maintained by St. Paul's Lutheran Church in Lohman reveal that the Jahreis family were active members of the congregation, and this church is where their son and three oldest daughters were confirmed. Some of the Jahreis children would also attend parochial school at St. Paul's but, in later years, went to Enterprise School—a local one-room schoolhouse—before having to walk into Russellville for high school.

For many years, Adam Jahreis would hitch a spring wagon to his horses for any traveling the family needed to do, but in 1915, he purchased a Dodge touring car, providing them a more comfortable journey. Sometime around the mid-1920s, the Jahreis family transferred their membership to Trinity Lutheran Church in Russellville, where their youngest daughter was confirmed.

"[Adam Jahreis] became a farmer and purchased property south of Russellville on Tellman Road," said Candace Stockton. "My mother [Hulda Loesch] was the second oldest of his four daughters and said that they first lived in a log cabin on the farm, but sometime around 1910, I believe, her parents built a brick home that still stands."

In her later years, Hulda Loesch penned a few reflections about growing up in the Jahreis home. She explained, "We were brought up by very strict parents [and were not] allowed to make much noise when papa was around as he always said children should be seen and not heard—an old German rule. We all had to be on time for every meal unless we had a very good excuse for not being there on time. After breakfast, we always had our daily devotions….In the evening after supper, Bible reading followed by the Lord's Prayer in unison by all family members."

As the years passed and the Jahreis children married and began having their own children, spending time on the farm with the grandparents became the recipe for many interesting memories for grandchildren like Candace Stockton.

"While I was growing up, I remember we would go visit Grandpa [Adam] Jahreis, and he would always speak German around the house," said Stockton. "My parents didn't want him to teach it to me because this was after World War II and it was not popular to speak German at that time."

Another memory Stockton recalls is the caring and generous nature of her grandparents, as demonstrated through how they treated family members in need. In later years, two of her grandmother's sisters lived in the Jahreis home since one suffered a physical impairment and the other, who had been living in Nebraska, was childless and had lost her husband.

A handwritten document found in some personal effects of the family notes of Adam and Rosina Jahreis, "In 1949, the couple observed [their]

Prior to emigrating from Bavaria, Jahreis was required to complete a three-year stint of training and service in the Bavarian army. Candace Stockton.

golden wedding jubilee. While blessed with good health throughout life, the departed complained about certain weaknesses, which advance in years." Clarifying details of Adam's death, the letter further details, "Doing some work in the hay loft, he died suddenly Saturday, June 27, 1953."

Adam Jahreis was laid to rest in Trinity Lutheran Cemetery near Russellville; his wife was ninety-three years old when she joined him in eternal glory in 1965.

"He was my grandfather, and I enjoyed spending time with him when I was younger," Stockton said. "I wouldn't say he was a 'warm and fuzzy' type of grandpa—it was the German in him, and they didn't tend to show emotion." She added, "But he loved God and his family, and would talk to me about things going on in my life, leaving me with many good memories."

During Jahreis's funeral, Pastor John Jacob Haberaecker remarked, "His devotion to our Trinity [Lutheran] Church is well known. To attend services in God's home regularly and to be a guest quite frequently at the Lord's table was to him a matter of primary importance."

WILLIAM SCHMOEGER

In October 1918, shortly before the armistice that brought an end to World War I and in the midst of the Spanish influenza pandemic, twenty-three-year-old William Schmoeger purchased a farm northwest of Russellville from his uncle. Now, more than a century later, his grandchildren continue to operate the historic farm, striving to preserve its Schmoeger family legacy for generations to come. Born in 1895 and raised on a farm south of Russellville, William Schmoeger's father passed away when he was quite young. His mother later remarried and continued to raise her children in the Lutheran faith.

"Our grandfather, William Schmoeger, purchased the 105-acre farm for $8,000 from his uncle, John Jungmeyer (his mother's brother) in October 1918," said Dwight Schmoeger. "The following January, he married our

William Schmoeger married Louise Plochberger in January 1919. Three months previously, William purchased from his uncle a farm northwest of Russellville that became known as Rainbow Valley Farm. *The Schmoeger family.*

grandmother, Louise Plochberger, of Lohman. They lived in a house on the farm that was built in 1907, and our father was at one time told that it cost John Jungmeyer $700 to build."

Donn Schmoeger, another of William's grandsons, went on to explain that there was once an old log home that also stood on the farm, although no one is certain when it was built. This house was later moved down a hill from its original location and used for many years as storage but was later demolished because of deterioration. William and Louise began to grow their family, yet not in the absence of tragedy. They would go on to become parents to four children—Ruth, Wilbert, Edna and Wanda. Sadly, both Edna and Wanda died in childhood. As the years passed, the Schmoeger farm garnered the name of Rainbow Valley Farm in recognition of the colorful ribbons that frequently painted the skies above.

West of the family home stands a barn, a section of which is believed to have been built in 1907. The barn was later added onto and has been used to store hay, corn and grain. In the lower section, stalls were created for horses and cattle, while dairy cows were milked inside the barn during the bitter weeks of winter.

Grinning and pointing to a small structure a short distance northwest of the house, Donn Schmoeger remarked, "That is the old outhouse...and it was a two-holer, meaning that two people were able to use it at the same time."

Other structures on the property include a smokehouse, woodshed, summer kitchen, chicken house and a windmill, which was used to pump water from a well. William was active in his community, serving as a director of the former Exchange Bank in Russellville in the years prior to the Great Depression.

The nearby Van Pool School—one of the many one-room schoolhouses that once stood in the area—was located near the farm and is where the children of William and Louise received their early education. For many years, William volunteered to serve on the school board in addition to being active with the Moniteau County Farm Bureau.

William's only son, Wilbert, was drafted in World War II and spent a couple of months training with the army in Alabama. He soon received a discharge because he was the only son of a farmer and agricultural products were a critical resource during the war. Shortly thereafter, on August 28, 1946, Wilbert married Irene Schock, and the couple went on to raise four sons (Bill, Donn, Dwight and John) and two daughters (Kathy Koestner and Brenda Stutte). They all came of age in the home that had been built in 1907 by Wilbert's great-uncle, John Jungmeyer.

In 1947, modern conveniences began to arrive when electricity came through the property. The farm continued to provide for the family, and in 1954, improvements to the home were made that included the digging of a basement and the installation of indoor plumbing.

"Dad said that our grandfather put a lock on the smokehouse door during the Great Depression because people roaming the countryside would come and help themselves to whatever meat was stored inside," said John Schmoeger.

Dwight mirthfully recalled, "Our grandfather purchased sixty wooded acres off Van Pool Road, where the school was located, because he was afraid of running out of firewood."

William Schmoeger passed away in 1963, and his wife joined him in eternal rest eighteen years later; both are interred in Trinity Lutheran Cemetery near Russellville. Wilbert, with the help of his wife and six

Wilbert Schmoeger is pictured with his wife, Irene Schock, in their wedding photograph from 1946. *The Schmoeger family.*

children, took over farming on Rainbow Valley Farm, a property that has grown to encompass 360 acres.

Like his father before him, Wilbert also served on the board of directors for the Community Bank of Russellville, which has since become Community Point Bank. In 1995, Wilbert's wife, Irene, passed away, and he followed her in eternal rest in 2010. Like his parents, they were laid to rest in Trinity Lutheran Cemetery.

The Rainbow Valley Farm continues to operate through a partnership between Wilbert and Irene Schmoeger's children. The family hosted a celebration on June 16, 2018, in recognition of its designation as a Century Farm, which was attended by an impressive 120 relatives and friends.

"We've walked every foot of the 360 acres and know just about every crevice and valley," said Donn Schmoeger.

Dwight Schmoeger added, "Here we are, more than a century later, and the grandchildren of William and Louise continue to cooperatively operate the farm. We, as a family, intend to preserve it for decades to come and hope that it can maintain its Schmoeger lineage."

CHAPTER 11

FRIEDENS CHURCH BRAZITO

*A Congregation Emerging from the Influence
of Zion Lutheran Church*

Churches often become historical representatives of the communities in which they are organized. Friedens United Church of Christ in Brazito, though small in membership, has weathered the decades with fortitude and continues to carry forth spiritual traditions that were established by its congregation's forebears around the beginning of the twentieth century.

On December 25, 1846, the Battle of El Brazito was fought between Missouri volunteers and Mexican troops along a bend in the Rio Grande during the Mexican-American War. The victory of the Missouri soldiers became etched in the memory of a veteran who returned to Cole County and, in the early 1850s, gave the name of this battle—Brazito—to the small community now located south of Jefferson City along US Highway 54.

Christopher Arnhold, a German immigrant and area landowner who is recognized for the founding of Brazito, erected a successful general store in the community. Soon, the community's population grew to more than four dozen residents, and it boasted such businesses and organizations as a post office, a hotel, a one-room schoolhouse, a blacksmith, a barbershop and fraternal lodges.

But it was Arnhold's only son, Charles, who took over his father's business endeavors and, through his generosity, helped bring a church to the community. As a charter member of the congregation, he donated the land on which the church was to be built.

Located along US Highway 54 in Brazito, Friedens Church Brazito remains a small congregation with a rich history. The church was organized in 1902 through the efforts of a pastor at Central Church in Jefferson City. *Jeremy P. Amick.*

Church records describe attempts to organize a church in Brazito beginning on September 1, 1889. Official minutes from Central Church in Jefferson City indicate that on this date, Rev. J.U. Schneider "was given permission to cancel one evening service each month in order to enable him to organize a Christian congregation in Brazito."

Despite Schneider's efforts, another thirteen years passed before his vision became a reality through the dedication of another pastor from Central Church.

"On October 19, 1902 [the official founding date], another service of worship was held in the Odd Fellows Hall [in Brazito] and a congregation was organized," church records reveal. "The group voted to erect a church edifice in the near future and hired Mr. Andy Miller as carpenter."

The Evangelical Friedens Church was organized under the leadership of Rev. Charles Hoffman. Translated from German, the word *frieden* means "peace." The name of the new church paid homage to the German families who helped establish it. In early summer 1903, the cornerstone for the new church was laid, and on November 22, 1903, the building was dedicated. In the year 1904, a site was designated for the church cemetery during a congregational meeting and the first full-time pastor, Rev. Martin Hoefer, was installed. In 1906, a parsonage was built on the northeast corner of the church property.

Although efforts to establish Friedens began in 1889, it was the dedication of Rev. Charles Hoffman that helped it become a reality in 1902. *Friedens Church Brazito.*

"In the early history of the congregation it was voted to become affiliated with what was then the German Evangelical Synod of North America," church historical documents explain.

Many forms of growth—spiritual, membership and church activities— defined the next few decades. Children's confirmation began in 1905, followed by erection of a parsonage and establishment of a Sunday school. Though businesses began to disappear from the Brazito landscape, the church remained a stalwart fixture.

"On April 1, 1951, the [nearby] Osage Bluff Methodist Church congregation which had ceased to function, decided to dispose of the church edifice," noted the Cole County Historical Society and Museum.

The congregation of Friedens purchased the Methodist church building for $300, and it was dismantled, moved and rebuilt in the back of the original Friedens Church to be used as a fellowship hall. Seven of the former Methodist church members transferred their membership to Friedens.

Throughout the years, Friedens has been identified by several different names, eventually becoming Friedens United Church of Christ in 1957. The naming was associated with changes in synodical affiliation, one of the more recent being its union with the Congregational Christian Churches, the United Church of Christ. The church no longer has an association with the United Church of Christ and is now known as Friedens Church Brazito.

The years were accompanied by improvements and updates to the church, with stained glass windows installed, a new altar placed and rooms added for

In 1906, a parsonage was built on the northeast corner of the church property and stood for nearly sixty-five years. *Friedens Church Brazito.*

Sunday school classes and new kitchen facilities. The parsonage, having stood for nearly sixty-five years, was razed in 1971.

The community of Brazito, though a relative shadow of its early, active self, gathered to participate in the country's bicentennial celebration activities in 1976. A monument made from native stone was built on the church grounds and contained a plaque honoring the community's history; the dedication took place on June 19, 1977.

"There really aren't any of the old-timers left who can tell the story of Brazito or Friedens," said Randy Deuschle. "My wife grew up in this church and was the great-granddaughter of John Bachmann, a charter member." Pausing, he added, "It's good to see the church continue its ministry and its history preserved."

Many longtime church members refer to the congregation as their second home, warmly recalling past members, such as the late Emmeline Crede. She and her husband, Clarence, were known for being active in the church and welcoming new and potential members to the congregation. The church has experienced varying levels of attendance, now averaging around thirty congregants at worship services. Its future, according to "A Brief History of Friedens United Church of Christ," compiled in 1977, is one built on a strong foundation by a dedicated and resourceful congregation.

The church history proclaims, "It is exciting to stand on the threshold of the future for Friedens, because with that kind of a past, anything can happen as the members continue to build the Kingdom of God in the neighborhood of Brazito."

CHARLES ARNHOLD

Business was booming in Brazito with the establishment of a blacksmith shop, sawmills, mining operations, a dance hall and physicians. Charles Arnhold soon added a hotel area to the general store and was later appointed to fulfill the role of postmaster, a position that had years earlier been held by his father.

Yet any joy that he may have experienced regarding his business success was tempered by the passing of his young wife, the former Theresa Guenther, in 1891. The same year, his father, Christopher Arnhold, a founding member of Zion Lutheran Church, also died. The elder Arnhold and his daughter-in-law are interred in a small burial ground in Brazito established for the Arnhold family.

Charles Arnhold's youngest son, Hugo, who was only two years old when his mother died, later received training in mercantilism and eventually assisted his father in the operation of their general store.

According to the *State Republican* newspaper in its edition from April 19, 1894, Charles Arnhold was not only actively committed to making updates to his store but had also embarked on an expansion of his business portfolio.

"Mr. C.A. Arnhold is improving the looks of his store. He is putting up a new hitching post," the newspaper reported. "Parties wishing to see $1,000 colts call at C.A. Arnhold's stables."

The following year, Charles Arnhold made newspaper headlines when, as reported the *State Republican* on January 31, 1895, he contracted with local men to "chop for him forty or fifty cords of wood." The article further explained, "It looks as though…Arnhold does not want to freeze this winter for he is having a lot of choppers and sawers do the work for him."

Just as his father had helped establish Zion Lutheran Church near Jefferson City decades earlier, in 1902, Charles Arnhold became a charter and organizing member of what is now Friedens Church Brazito. His background in business earned him the appointment as the congregation's first treasurer in a meeting held at the community's Odd Fellows Hall.

Charles Arnhold is pictured with his wife, Theresa. His father, Christopher, was a Prussian immigrant who established a store in Brazito and was a founding member of Zion Lutheran Church. Years later, Charles helped found Friedens Church in Brazito. *Friedens Church Brazito.*

The church and subsequent cemetery were erected on property conveyed from Arnhold to the trustees of the new "German Evangelical Welcome Friedens Church." Early church records written in German reveal that Arnhold's son, Hugo, was confirmed at the church in 1905.

The sixty-one-year-old Charles Arnhold passed away on June 2, 1917, and is interred alongside his wife in the family cemetery in Brazito. The church continued to grow throughout the decades and remains an enduring fixture in the community. However, the ownership of Arnhold's store changed hands several times in the intervening decades, and it has since been torn down, remaining little more than a faded memory. In 1976, Shirley Nelson drew pictures of Brazito's past, including one featuring the Arnhold Store. These pictures were used for the Brazito Bicentennial Quilt now at the Cole County Historical Society.

"There may have been a time when preservation was about saving an old building here and there, but those days are gone," said Richard Moe, a historic preservationist. "Preservation is in the business of saving communities and the values they embody."

When traveling down Highway 54 through Brazito, one may witness little more than a fleeting glimpse into the past. However, this community continues to embody the visionary spirit of Christopher Arnhold; his son, Charles; and other forgotten families who came to this country seeking to build a better life for all and contributing to the noble cause of humanity.

JOHN BACHMANN

Johann Bauschmann was born on January 4, 1847, in an area of northern Switzerland known as Swabia. This region also encompassed parts of what are now eastern France and southwestern Germany, serving as home to a people possessing a unique history, culture and German-based dialect. The Swabians earned a reputation for being both thrifty and tidy, in addition to possessing an affinity for their beers and wines. Their orderly instincts were also reflected through industriousness, giving birth to sundry inventors, including Albert Einstein and Carl Benz, the latter of whom joined Gottlieb Daimler in establishing what became Mercedes-Benz.

When only nineteen years old, Bauschmann emigrated from his European homeland and eventually settled in the Brazito area, enmeshing himself in a community that was experiencing an unprecedented period of growth. It was here that he embarked on a lifelong career in agriculture and helped establish a church that continues to serve the local community.

"Sometime after he came to the Brazito area, he changed his name to John Bachmann, possibly to sound more German since there were so many Germans who had settled in the area," said Randy Deuschle, whose late wife, Carolyn, was a great-granddaughter of Bachmann.

Bachmann embraced the productive reputation of the Swabians when choosing to become a farmer. According to the Cole County plat map from 1914, his farm grew to encompass more than 166 acres. On June 4, 1868, two years following his immigration to Missouri, Bachmann was married in Cole County to Barbara Meisel, a native of Bavaria. As the years passed, he and his wife raised two sons and a daughter while becoming actively involved in the Brazito community.

"[Christopher] Arnhold began merchandising in Jefferson City in 1866 and the following year moved his stock of goods to Brazito," explains *Godspeed's Cole County History* from 1889. "In 1880, he sold a one-half interest to his son Charles, and in 1885 the latter became sole proprietor."

Christopher Arnhold, a Prussian immigrant originally of the Lutheran faith, passed away in 1891 and was laid to rest in a plot on property owned by his family. His son, Charles, was joined by John Bachmann and eight others for a service at the Odd Fellows Hall in Brazito on October 19, 1902, for the purpose of organizing a new congregation in the area.

"On January 25, 1903, the newly organized congregation held its first business meeting and elected the following to serve as members of the Official Church Board: John J. Weber and Philip Blochberger for a period of one year, and Daniel Schrieber and John Bachmann to serve for a period of two years," notes a brief history of Friedens United Church of Christ.

With a new church now being established in Brazito, an area for a church cemetery was designated in 1904. The same year, Bachmann's wife passed away; hers was one of the first burials in the cemetery. Records maintained by the congregation reveal that Bachmann, a dedicated member of what was initially named the German Evangelical Friedens Church, was not of a personality to shy away from difficult tasks.

John Bachmann immigrated to Brazito in 1866 from an area in Europe known as Swabia. He went on to become a farmer and was active in the establishment of what became Friedens Church Brazito. *Friedens Church Brazito.*

"In the early history of the congregation, the Church Board appointed one or more persons to collect the pastor's salary," recorded an unknown historian in church records. "Mr. John Bachmann was the first member to be given that responsibility. He was also the first lay delegate of the congregation to attend what is now called the Missouri Conference Meeting. At that time, it was called a conference of the West Missouri District."

While toiling to make a living on his nearby farm, Bachmann remained actively involved in affairs of the church. He volunteered on a building committee that resulted in the construction of not only the first church building but also a parsonage a few years later. The parsonage was dedicated at Friedens Church Brazito in 1907 and remained standing until it was demolished in 1971.

As a man of agriculture who had erected barns on his own property, Bachmann helped build a barn for their pastor's horse in 1907. Each member of the congregation was "placed under the obligation to furnish two dollars' worth of feed per year for the horse," church records note.

The following year, Bachmann demonstrated his financial wherewithal when working with ten members of the congregation to sell bonds in order to secure the church against loss.

Although he did not personally witness the Civil War due to arriving after the end of the conflict, Bachmann read the news of the United States' entry into World War I and celebrated with others when word of the armistice reached the Brazito community. The Spanish influenza exploded into an unfortunate scourge during this timeframe, resulting in the closures of churches and other public places. Regrettably, Bachmann succumbed to the flu on March 16, 1919, two months after having reached seventy-two years of age. He was laid to rest in the cemetery at the church he had helped establish less than two decades earlier.

"People come here penniless but not cultureless," writes American psychologist Mary Pipher. "They bring us gifts. We can synthesize the best of our traditions with the best of theirs. We can teach and learn from each other to produce a better America."

The positive legacy that Bachmann left in the Brazito community continues to resonate with the church he so adored and to which he devoted so much of his love and effort.

"He still has descendants that are members of Friedens Church Brazito," said Randy Deuschle. "Through the church and its continued ministry, his story—and that of many others from the early days of Brazito—continues to live on."

JOHN ASEL

The story of John Gottlieb Asel parallels that of many children of immigrant families making their journey to Missouri in the mid-1800s. Many of these individuals, inspired by the bold, pioneering spirit demonstrated by their parents, carved out a living in their new homes and went on to build businesses while strengthening the rural communities in which they settled.

John Michael Asel emigrated from his native Saxony (Germany) in 1849 and, while traveling to the United States, met Margaretta Mueller aboard the ship. On their arrival in New York, the two parted ways until fate reunited them several weeks later.

"One Sunday morning…Margaretta, seated in a church pew in the capital city [Washington, D.C.] of her adopted homeland, was startled by a tap upon her shoulder," wrote Chares E. Dewey in a July 8, 1946 article for the *Sunday News and Tribune*. "Who in this strange land would approach her? Turning, her amazement gave way to join in the recognition of her ship companion, John Asel. Such a coincidence could lead to but one result—to romance, and so Margaretta and John were married in Washington County and their first child, John (Gottlieb) was born there [in 1852]."

John M. Asel soon fell ill, motivating his decision to move to Jefferson City with his young wife and their young son in hopes of improving his health. Settling in a small log house near the junction of Ashley and Madison Streets, the immigrant family grew by several children in the coming years. The family befriended local Native Americans, many of whom developed a fondness for Margaretta's homemade breads, baked in a large outdoor oven.

Born to German immigrants in 1852, John Gottlieb Asel was raised in Jefferson City. He later became a clerk for a local businessman before moving to the settlement southwest of Jefferson City known as Bass, where he operated a general mercantile. *Friedens Church Brazito.*

"During the Civil War, the Asels made considerable money selling sausage sandwiches to the soldiers," explained an article in the July 6, 1964 *Washington Citizen*. "Increasing numbers of Jefferson City residents came to purchase fresh, cured and cooked meats."

This soon grew into a family business of meat processing, providing a young John Gottlieb Asel with experience that would transition into a mercantile career. In the 1870s, he became a clerk for William H. Morlock, also the son of German immigrants, who had established a successful general merchandise operation in Jefferson City.

In 1877, John Gottlieb Asel was united in marriage to Johannah E. Bohnenberger. Her father, Michael Bohnenberger, was a farmer who also owned a store and saloon in Stringtown. The year following their marriage, John purchased his own general mercantile store in Jefferson City. Asel and his wife welcomed five daughters and a son in the coming years. In the late 1880s, he made the decision to leave Jefferson City, moving his family several miles south near the small community of Brazito and embarking on a career in mercantile management.

"Mr. John G. Asel, manager of the Co-Operative Association store at Brazito, is a popular and prominent man in business circles and will add much to its success," explained the *State Republican* on July 10, 1890.

The following year, John became manager of a store in another nearby settlement. Bass was located between Brazito and Hickory Hill near Old Bass

Road, along what is now US Highway 54, and was best known for a small store established by a group of local farmers. A post office was established in the store in 1890, at which time the little community received its designation. The settlement was named for Metheldred Bass Sr., a farmer who owned a large tract of property in the area.

"A few miles from Brazito and we come to Bass; here the F. & L.U. have a large cooperative store; it is under the gentlemanly management of our old friend, John Asel who, together with his assistants, is kept busy all day by waiting on customers," reported the *State Republican* on February 19, 1891.

Asel's political leanings were aligned with the Republican party. In 1892, he vocalized his support for William Warner, a Civil War veteran and Kansas City mayor running for the office of governor of Missouri. Warner, who campaigned on the slogan "A New Missouri," lost the election to the Democratic nominee, former congressman William Stone.

In 1902, Asel became a charter member of the German Evangelical Welcome Friedens Church in Brazito (now Friedens Church Brazito). With business continuing to increase in the community of Bass, Asel eventually purchased the Bass Mercantile Company. However, unexpected tragedy brought an abrupt closure to his mercantile endeavors.

"John G. Asel, a merchant residing at Bass...committed suicide today by shooting himself with a .22-caliber rifle," reported the *Kansas City Times* on December 13, 1912. "He had been in business there...and was in good circumstances."

The body of the sixty-year-old Asel was laid to rest in the Central Evangelical Church Cemetery in Jefferson City, where his parents were interred. In 1965, his remains were among those relocated to Riverview Cemetery to make way for the expansion of US Highway 54. Soon after Asel's death, his widow, Johannah, moved to Kansas City, where her son, Otto, was employed as an optometrist for the Goldman Jewelry Company. She died in 1946 and was buried in Highland Park Cemetery in Kansas City, Kansas.

In her book *The Invisible Life of Addie LaRue*, V.E. Schwab writes, "It is sad, of course, to forget. But it is a lonely thing, to be forgotten. To remember when no one else does."

The post office closed in 1913, and Bass soon faded from the maps. The mercantile building was eventually demolished, and only muted whispers of a once-eventful settlement remain. Asel and the community he helped grow have receded from the landscape but represent fascinating historical moments worthy of commemoration.

CHAPTER 12

FAITH LUTHERAN CHURCH

(JEFFERSON CITY)

*A New Church Planted from the Congregation
of Trinity Lutheran Church*

In 1870, Pastor Carl Thurow, who was serving as pastor of Zion Lutheran Church, established the first Lutheran congregation in Jefferson City with the organization of Trinity Lutheran Church. Eighty years later, following exponential growth of the church body, a new congregation known as Faith Lutheran Church was established on the west end of the city. This newer congregation has been affiliated with the Missouri Synod–Lutheran Church since its founding and remains the youngest church of this synod in Cole County.

"In 1950, a group of members of Trinity Lutheran Church, then under the pastorate of the Rev. Alfred C. Schmalz, asked for release in order to form a new congregation," explains the fiftieth anniversary booklet of Faith Lutheran Church.

Trinity Lutheran Church was in 1950 located on the northwest corner of Monroe and McCarty Streets. Its leadership recognized that their fifty-one-year-old church building, limited in size and often requiring repair, could no longer sustain its massive congregation.

"Approval was granted, and Trinity gave the group $25,000 with which to begin the new mission," the booklet clarifies. "At that time, Trinity numbered about 1,200 souls and 199 of these were released to begin the new congregation on April 11, 1950." Of this charter group, 145 were communicants and 54 children."

Faith Lutheran Church is the youngest of the Missouri Synod Lutheran churches in Cole County. It was established in 1950 by 199 members released from Trinity Lutheran Church in Jefferson City. *Jeremy P. Ämick.*

A ten-year anniversary publication explains, "By popular vote, the new congregation was aptly named 'Faith' to express the group's faith in God and the future in the challenging task which lay before them."

Church records note that the first congregational president of Faith Lutheran was Theodore Engelbrecht, along with Arthur Heisinger as vice president, Herbert Harfst as secretary and Harry Goldammer as treasurer.

Larry Meisel, who was nine years old when his family became charter members of Faith Lutheran Church, recalls making the transfer from Trinity to help start the new congregation.

"The building that the church moved into had previously been the fan factory for Wren Manufacturing Company, located where U.S. Bank is now on the corner of Dix Road and Industrial Drive," he said. "We have an aerial photo showing that all that was in the area at the time was a nearby house, ballfields and farmland," he added.

While remodeling was underway to make their new church home useable, arrangements were made to conduct temporary services at nearby West School. A chapel, measuring twenty-eight by one hundred feet, was built in the basement of the former factory building, and the dedicatory service held there on June 5, 1950. The dedicatory service for the new church was led by Rev. E. Bultmann of Immanuel Lutheran Church in Honey Creek. On

July 30, 1950, Rev. William Wollenburg was installed as Faith's first pastor. For eleven years, Wollenburg helped bolster the growing congregation until accepting a call to St. Paul's Lutheran Church in Concordia, Missouri.

By 1952, the church body of Faith had grown in size by one third and numbered 303 members, 96 of whom were children. In 1954, a second story was added to be used as a Christian day school for the first through eighth grades. This decision was inspired by overcrowding at Trinity's school and because many of Faith's members believed tuition being paid for their children to attend Trinity could instead be used to build and sustain their own school.

"A new sanctuary, fellowship hall, classrooms and an office wing were built on the property in 1962, but the school remained in the old factory building," said Henry Gensky, another charter member of Faith.

This construction endeavor occurred during the tenure of Rev. Norman C. Meyer, second pastor for Faith Lutheran, who was succeed by Rev. Arthur Graf in September 1967. Then, in 1971, Rev. James W. Kalthoff was installed around the time the decision was made to close the Christian school.

Pictured is Pastor Alfred Schmalz of Trinity Lutheran Church of Jefferson City leading the congregation of the newly founded Faith Lutheran Church into their new worship area in 1950. *Faith Lutheran Church.*

"The congregation decided to sell the school building and a small piece of property in 1973 to Missouri Bank," said Larry Meisel. "The money received from that sale was used to pay off the debt of the earlier church construction and helped us begin another building project."

A new educational wing and a gymnasium were dedicated in 1976. The church continued to thrive throughout the next several years with the hiring of a director of Christian education and the organization of a weekday school and preschool.

"We went through another major building program and added an educational wing with classrooms in 2005," said Larry Meisel. "A sound Christian education for our youth has always been a priority of the congregation from the beginning."

Several full-time and interim pastors would serve in the pulpit at Faith in the years that followed Pastor Kalthoff's departure in 1991. Through it all, the congregation embraced a steady growth in membership. In the year 2000, the once-small congregation that had begun with the planting of 199 initial members coming from Trinity Lutheran Church had flourished into a large congregation with more than 900 members.

As a descendant of early German immigrants to the community, Larry Meisel recognizes that Faith does not possess the extensive historical legacy of many Lutheran churches in the county. However, despite its youth, Faith has been blessed with growth throughout the years and remains deeply involved in congregational outreach.

"One of the things I have noticed about Faith Lutheran Church, since I became a charter member in 1950, is that we are really a friendly church," he said. "And I'm not saying that there are unfriendly congregations, but here it seems like people go out of their way to introduce themselves to visitors and welcome them. We might not have the history of other churches, but I consider the congregation of Faith a close family, and that has been part of the reason for our continued growth throughout the years."

CHAPTER 13

OUR SAVIOR'S LUTHERAN CHURCH

(JEFFERSON CITY)

Springing Forth from the Congregations at Russellville and Lohman

I n the years following World War II, many younger people began
leaving their rural upbringings and moved to Jefferson City to embark
on their careers. A number of these individuals belonged to Lutheran
congregations in Russellville and Lohman that were at the time affiliated with
a synod that has since become the Evangelical Lutheran Church of America.
Although several continued to make the trip of several miles to these smaller
communities to attend worship services, a small group of these Lutherans
resolved to organize a new congregation closer to their homes in the city.

"A new congregation of the…Lutheran Church is now being formed
here," reported the *Jefferson City Post Tribune* on July 10, 1959. "The Rev.
Edward R. Baack has moved from Pittsburg, Kansas, to a parsonage at…
Mesa Ave., to supervise work in the new mission church, tentatively named
Our Savior's Lutheran Church."

In a letter dated August 5, 1959, extending an invitation to participate in
the organization of the new church, Pastor Edward Baack wrote, "The first
service will be held this coming Sunday, August 9th, in the McClung Park
Recreational Hall at 10:30 a.m.…We will worship in the Park until the first
unit of our church is completed."

An estimated eighty people attended this first worship service. After
receiving a subsidy for operating expenses provided by the Mission
Committee of the Central District of the American Lutheran Church, Our
Savior's Lutheran Church was officially organized on December 13, 1959.

Pastor Howard Hahn, at the time serving as pastor of St. Paul's
Lutheran Church in Lohman, along with William Gemeinhardt, traveled

around the Jefferson City area to locate an adequate property for the new church building.

"Plans for construction of the church started immediately after the organization took place," explains the tenth anniversary booklet printed in 1969. "The groundbreaking service was on May 22, 1960, and the dedication of the sanctuary at 1529 Southwest Boulevard was on November 13, 1960." The booklet adds, "Until this time, the congregation had continued to meet at the recreation pavilion at McClung Park."

Shortly after Our Savior's Lutheran Church organized, it earned the designation as the youngest congregation in the new American Lutheran Church (ALC). The ALC was formed during a convention held in Minneapolis in the spring of 1960, where the earlier iteration of the ALC, the Evangelical Lutheran Church and the United Evangelical Lutheran Church merged.

During the summer of 1960, Otto Schramm and his wife, the sole remaining members of the former Lutheran church congregation in Centertown, donated their church bell to Our Savior's Lutheran Church. The bell was used during special occasions for many years by the Jefferson City congregation and, after a recent renovation, is now prominently displayed near the main entrance.

The congregation of Our Savior's received a $60,000 loan because of the graciousness of St. John's Lutheran Church of Beatrice, Nebraska, whose congregation offered their church property as collateral. This loan was later refinanced locally through Exchange National Bank.

"The first unit will consist primarily of a chapel seating 120 persons, with overflow facilities to accommodate 40 additional persons," noted the *Jefferson City Post-Tribune* on February 5, 1960, describing early church construction. "The building will also house the church office and a general activities area in the basement will double for classrooms and for fellowship functions."

Plans for the contemporary structure were prepared by the architecture firm of Hollis & Miller of Overland Park, Kansas. The construction contract was awarded to the Roy Scheperle Construction Company, which also built the new Trinity Lutheran Church in Jefferson City around the same timeframe.

In the span of a decade, a congregation that had begun with 37 confirmed members and 57 baptized grew to 156 confirmed and 220 baptized. From its founding in 1959 until January 1967, Rev. Edward Baack served as pastor for Our Savior's Lutheran Church, at which time he accepted a call to a church of the same name in Lincoln, Nebraska.

Left: The bell from the former Lutheran church in Centertown was donated to Our Savior's Lutheran Church in 1960 and is now displayed outside the church. *Our Savior's Lutheran Church.*

Below: Born in Russellville and confirmed in Trinity Lutheran Church there, Hugo Goldammer was a charter member of Our Savior's Lutheran Church. He is pictured with his wife, Esther, and their son, Michael. *Our Savior's Lutheran Church.*

"The Rev. Harold J. Laursen accepted the call to be the new pastor," a church history notes. "Pastor and Mrs. Laursen and their children, Kathryn, Elizabeth, and James arrived on March 1, 1967, from Kennard, Nebraska." Laursen was succeeded by Rev. Robert F. Klein Sr., who was installed in May 1973. During Klein's tenure, additions were made to the church to include classrooms and increased sanctuary space.

In the summer of 1988, a new sanctuary was dedicated on the north end of the original church building. Parts of the original church were converted into storage, classrooms and office space. It was also in 1988 that Our Savior's became part of the Evangelical Lutheran Church of America following the merger of three Lutheran church groups.

After Rev. Klein's departure in 1994, the congregation of Our Savior's was served by an interim pastor for one year prior to the installation of Rev. Dr. Scott Musselman, who continues to serve the congregation.

"There is a house next to the church that one of our members purchased years ago and then donated to the church," said Stan Linsenbardt, who has fulfilled the role of president, treasurer and bookkeeper in past years. "Now it's being used as housing for one of our members and for storage," he added.

Art Firley, who lived in Germany as a youth and was drafted into the German army when only sixteen years old, later came to the United States and served in the army during the Korean War. He became financially successful as the president of the Casualty Indemnity Exchange insurance company in Jefferson City but was best known as a philanthropist who supported many religious and civic organizations. He became an active member of Our Savior's Lutheran Church and served stints as the president of the congregation.

Though possessing only a brief history when compared to other area churches, Our Savior's Lutheran has grown from a small seed into a bustling congregation in a short period of time.

"A faithful core of Christians have worked diligently in the evangelistic outreach of the congregation and have supported the financial program with sacrificial gifts," notes the bulletin from the church's tenth anniversary celebration in 1969.

And just as other churches influenced the establishment of Our Savior's Lutheran Church, the anniversary booklet describes a hope that the spiritual influence of the congregation will extend outside the church walls: "We pray that the Communion of Saints they experienced while members of Our Savior's Lutheran Church has enriched their spiritual lives so that the influence of [our church] is felt beyond the community of Jefferson City."

CHAPTER 14

PEACE LUTHERAN CHURCH
(JEFFERSON CITY)

Cole County's Youngest Lutheran Congregation, Born of Strife in the 1980s

Following a disagreement that unfolded during the mid-1980s at Immanuel Lutheran Church in Honey Creek, forty-two baptized church members made the decision to leave the congregation and explore the possibility of establishing a new church in the area. Through their dedication, this small group founded Peace Lutheran Church and created the only congregation in Cole County affiliated with the small Evangelical Lutheran Synod.

"At first, we really didn't know what to do," said Paul Junkans, whose father, Ervin, served many years as pastor for Immanuel Lutheran Church. "Should we go to another church, or do we start another church? We visited a church at the Lake before finally deciding that we were going to embark upon the process of forming a new church."

On July 10, 1986, the small group held its first unofficial meeting and, ten days later, met under an oak tree in the front yard of Tom and Lisa Ittner for their first worship service as a new church body.

"We were fortunate that it was a nice day, and we used *The Lutheran Hymnal* for songs, and Walter Henry Jr. played music on a small organ with an amplifier," said Junkans. "The sermon was read from Rev. Graf's sermon book." Rev. Arthur Graf was a longtime Missouri Synod pastor who had served many years at Faith Lutheran Church in Jefferson City.

Several of these Christians, seeking to establish their own permanent place of worship, traveled to Trinity Lutheran Church in New Haven, Missouri, to participate in their worship service. While there, they were advised that

A small group of Missouri Synod Lutherans gathered in 1986 to discuss establishing a new church. What came from this meeting is now Peace Lutheran Church, the newest Lutheran congregation in Cole County and a member of the Evangelical Lutheran Synod. *Jeremy P. Ämick.*

a retired pastor of the Lutheran Church—Missouri Synod (LCMS), might be able to assist them. The group applied for membership with the Missouri Synod and rented a place at the Capital Mall in Jefferson City to hold their services under the pastoral guidance of Rev. Luther Anderson. Meetings continued to discuss incorporating as a congregation with the State of Missouri, a process that was finalized on October 1, 1986.

"I believe it was Wanda Smith who came up with the name 'peace' to use for the church name, and that's how it came to be 'Peace Lutheran Church,'" said Junkans, who served as the first chairman of the church board.

However, the process of becoming affiliated with the Missouri Synod continued to be defined by challenges.

"I recall it was my own father (a Missouri Synod pastor) who said that we should look into affiliating with the Evangelical Lutheran Synod (ELS)," Junkans said. "The ELS president visited with us in February 1987 to discuss the structure of the ELS, doctrine and other such things. At a voters meeting, we decided to withdraw our application with the LCMS and apply to the ELS, with whom we did eventually become affiliated. Then, we were able to borrow the money to purchase property and build a church."

Utilizing the services of real estate agent Ben Rogers, the council of Peace Lutheran Church purchased eleven acres of property two miles north of

Brazito, which was locally referred to as the Aldo Kroeger property, for $23,000. Plans were drawn up for a one-hundred-person sanctuary and associated spaces.

Construction of the church began in late spring of 1987 while Pastor Anderson continued to serve the congregation. He departed in July, and the ELS president coordinated for an interim pastor to serve Peace Lutheran Church.

"The church dedication took place on November 8 [1987] and the following spring we had our first confirmation class," Junkans recalled. "We also began discussing the development of a cemetery on the property."

Church records indicate that the first interment in the cemetery of Peace Lutheran Church occurred in 1994 and was that of Crystal, the infant daughter of Bobby and Celeste Gilmore.

"An exciting moment in our early church history was the arrival of our first full-time pastor in July 1988, Pastor Micah Ernst, along with his wife, Claudia, and their children," Junkans said.

Embracing the pleasing circumstance of sustained congregational growth, ground was broken for a new 2,400-square-foot addition in October 2001. The addition became the new worship sanctuary, while the former sanctuary provides space for a fellowship hall. Much of the construction was made possible through numerous memorials and donations.

"We had three stained-glass windows installed in the sanctuary, and the congregation wanted to ensure they contained Christian symbolism," said Junkans. "The one to the left of the altar represents baptism, and the one on the right is about the Lord's supper." He added, "The one above the altar represents the word of God as the sword of the spirit."

Hanging on the wall inside the entrance to the sanctuary is a painting titled *Means of Grace* that was commissioned by Hannah Ernst, a talented artist and daughter of longtime Peace Lutheran pastor Micah Ernst. Pastor Ernst served the congregation of Peace Lutheran for eleven years until accepting a call to Ohio in 1999. Several pastors served the small congregation in the ensuing years. In December 2015, Pastor Ernst returned and continues to serve the congregation.

As part of his ministry, Pastor Ernst also serves Grace Lutheran Church in Columbia as part of a shared pastoral agreement.

The history of Peace Lutheran Church may appear but a fleeting moment when compared to the lengthy legacy of other Lutheran churches in the area, but as Junkans explained, it is through divine grace that their small Lutheran synod was planted and has flourished in the community.

Hannah Ernst, a talented artist and daughter of a longtime pastor of Peace Lutheran, was commissioned to create the painting *Means of Grace*, which now hangs in the church. *Jeremy P. Ämick.*

"Our congregation came out of strife as we are simply forgiven sinners, but the Holy Spirit continues to shine the light of Jesus among his people," he said. "We really like the synod we belong to, but ultimately the church is about seeking souls for Christ's kingdom and not the building. We want to stay true to our God and his Word…and share our hope in a loving way."

BIBLIOGRAPHY

Baepler, Walter A. *A Century of Grace: A History of the Missouri Synod, 1847–1947*. St. Louis, MO: Concordia Publishing House, 1947.

Bangs, Nathan. *The Reviewer Answered: Or the Discipline and Usages of the Methodist Episcopal Church, Defended Against the Attacks of the Christian Spectator.* New York: J. Emory & B. Waugh, 1830.

California Democrat. "New Marker for Old Centertown Cemetery." June 18, 2003.

Central United Church of Christ. *A Sesquicentennial History, 1858–2008*. Marceline, MO: Walsworth, 2008.

Daily Capital News. "Rich Memories Coming to End." October 9, 1975.

———. "Zion Church Marks 125th Anniversary." July 20, 1968.

Dau, W.H.T., ed. *Ebenezer: Reviews of the Work of the Missouri Synod during Three Quarters of a Century.* St. Louis, MO: Concordia Publishing House, 1922.

Faith Lutheran Church. *History of Faith Lutheran Church, 1950–1961*. Jefferson City, MO: self-published, 1961.

———. *Our Church 2000: Fifty Years in Faith by Grace*. Jefferson City, MO: self-published, 2000.

Forster, Walter O. *Zion on the Mississippi: The Settlement of the Saxon Lutherans in Missouri 1839–1841*. St. Louis, MO: Concordia Publishing House, 1953.

German Valley Bulletin. "St. John Lutheran Church, Pecatonica." August 3, 1956.

Humboldt Standard. "Funeral Services for Minister." June 1, 1934.

Illustrated Sketchbook & Directory of Jefferson City and Cole County, Missouri, 1900. United States: Capital City Family Research, 1900.

Jefferson City Post-Tribune. "American Lutheran Mission Being Formed Here." July 10, 1959.

———. "Preliminary Plans Approved for New Lutheran Building." February 5, 1960.

———. "60 Years of Lutheranism at Honey Creek." July 25, 1930.

———. "Society." November 26, 1934.

Kansas City Star. "The Republican Spirit of Missouri's German Pioneers." August 23, 1923.

Kansas City Times. "A Bass, Mo., Merchant Commits Suicide." December 13, 1912.

Magaret, E.C. *Jubiläumsbuch der St. Louis Deutschen Konferenz.* Cincinnati, OH: Jennings and Graham, 1906.

Meyer, Duane. *The Heritage of Missouri: A History.* St. Louis, MO: State Publishing, 1963.

Miller, Rev. Adam. *Experience of German Methodist Preachers.* Cincinnati, OH: Methodist Book Concern, 1859.

Oshkosh Northwestern. "Ex-Minister J.P. Koeller Dies at Bay." September 9, 1957.

Our Savior's Lutheran Church. *A Brief History of Our Savior's Lutheran Church.* Jefferson City, MO: self-published, 1979.

Proft, Robert, and George Nielsen. "Johann August Proft." *The Wendish Research Exchange.* April 2012. https://wendishresearch.org.

Ravenswaay, Charles V. *The Arts and Architecture of German Settlements in Missouri.* Columbia: University of Missouri Press, 1977.

Republican-Northwestern. "Former Belvidere Pastor Is Dead." October 15, 1918.

Scheperle, Palmer. *History of the Scheperle (Schepperle) Family of America.* Jefferson City, MO: Modern-Litho Print, 1982.

———. *Zion Lutheran Church Community Heritage and History of Cole County, Missouri.* Jefferson City, MO: self-published, n.d.

Schwab, V.E. *The Invisible Life of Addie LaRue.* New York, NY: Tor Books, 2020.

Stanton, Shelby L. *World War II Order of Battle.* New York: Galahad Books, 1984.

State Journal. "Important Decision." January 29, 1875.

Stevens, Walter B. *Centennial History of Missouri, 1820–1921.* Vol. 1. Chicago: S.J. Clarke Publishing, 1921.

St. John's Lutheran Church. *Fifty Years of Worship.* Stringtown, MO: self-published, 1955.

———. *Founded on the Rock, Forward in Faith, 150 Years: 1867–2017.* Jefferson City, MO: Brown Printing, 2017.

———. *100 Years of Boundless Grace, 1867–1967.* Jefferson City, MO: New Day Press, 1967.

St. Louis Post-Dispatch. "Former Missourian Would Unite Lutherans." August 20, 1899.

St. Paul's Evangelical Lutheran Church. *100th Anniversary, 1852–1952.* Lohman, MO: self-published, 1952.

———. *125th Anniversary: 1852–1977.* Lohman, MO: self-published, 1977.

———. *150th Anniversary Edition, 1852–2002.* Lohman, MO: self-published, 2002.

Sunday News and Tribune. "Honey Creek Lutheran Church Observes Anniversary." September 2, 1945.

———. "Lohman Veteran Walks 700 Miles in Two Years to Attend V.F.W. Meets." April 25, 1937.

———. "Lutheran Church of Zion Celebrates Centennial." July 25, 1943.

———. "Trying Days in Founding and Then Establishment of Local Church Are Recalled." October 29, 1933.

Trinity Evangelical Lutheran Church. *Golden Jubilee: 1895–1945.* Russellville, MO: self-published, 1945.

———. *Sixtieth Anniversary: 1895–1955.* Russellville, MO: self-published, November 13, 1955.

———. *Seventy-Fifth Anniversary: 1895–1970.* Russellville, MO: self-published, 1970.

Trinity Lutheran Church. *75 Years of Divine Blessing, 1870–1945.* Jefferson City, MO: self-published, 1945.

———. *Centennial, 1970.* Jefferson City, MO: self-published, 1970.

Trinity Lutheran Church & School. *150th Anniversary Commemoration, 1870–2020.* Jefferson City, MO: self-published, 2020.

Whitney, Carrie Westlake. *Kansas City, Missouri: Its History and Its People, 1800–1908.* Vol. 2. Chicago: S.J. Clarke Publishing, 1908.

Zion Lutheran Church. *One Hundredth Anniversary. 1843–1943.* Jefferson City, MO: self-published, 1943.

———. *125 Years Given to God's Mission.* Jefferson City, MO: self-published, 1968.

INDEX

ABOUT THE AUTHOR

J eremy P. Ämick, a veteran of the Missouri National Guard and U.S. Army, is a military historian and public affairs officer with the Silver Star Families of America and has for years strived to preserve the history of Missouri and its communities. Images were obtained from the author's personal collection and through generous donations from members of various Lutheran churches in and around Cole County.